Positive Endings in Psychotherapy

Steven Aaron Kramer

Positive Endings
in Psychotherapy

Bringing Meaningful Closure
to Therapeutic Relationships

 Jossey-Bass Publishers

San Francisco   •   Oxford   •   1990

POSITIVE ENDINGS IN PSYCHOTHERAPY
Bringing Meaningful Closure to Therapeutic Relationships
by Steven Aaron Kramer

Copyright © 1990 by: Jossey-Bass Inc., Publishers
350 Sansome Street
San Francisco, California 94104
&
Jossey-Bass Limited
Headington Hill Hall
Oxford OX3 0BW

Library of Congress Cataloging-in-Publication Data

Kramer, Steven Aaron, date.
Positive endings in psychotherapy : bringing meaningful closure to
therapeutic relationships / Steven Aaron Kramer.
p. cm. — (Jossey-Bass social and behavioral science series)
Includes bibliographical references.
ISBN 1-55542-258-6
1. Psychotherapy. I. Title. II. Series.
RC480.K695 1990
616.89′14—dc20   90-4491
                                                      CIP

Portions of this book contain excerpts from *August* by Judith Rossner.
Copyright © 1983 by Judith Rossner. Reprinted with permission from
Houghton Mifflin Company.

Manufactured in the United States of America

The paper in this book meets the guidelines for
permanence and durability of the Committee on
Production Guidelines for Book Longevity of the
Council on Library Resources.

JACKET DESIGN BY WILLI BAUM

FIRST EDITION

Code 9065

The Jossey-Bass
Social and Behavioral Science Series

Contents

Foreword

Undergoing intensive psychodynamic psychotherapy is deeply personal. For many individuals, this adventure into unknown recesses of their psyches reveals personal vistas previously unimagined. Such exploration frequently involves painful disclosures, frightening discoveries, an extraordinary development of self-understanding, an increase in capacity for intimate sharing, and an integration of strengths and aspirations. Such a journey, with phases of both pain and exhilaration, usually takes place over an extended period.

Since psychodynamic psychotherapy is often long and intimate, it is not surprising that the process of terminating such an experience is often complex and difficult for both clients and psychotherapists. Approaches to understanding the process of psychotherapy have been multidimensional, with intricate theories exploring both the dynamics of clients and those of therapists. The theorists of the past ninety years have attempted to focus on the process of treatment itself, its evolving stages, and the most troublesome problems encountered at each stage. Surprisingly little of the literature in the field has dealt with the actual ending of psychotherapy, the subject of this excellent book by Steven Aaron Kramer.

The discussion in *Positive Endings in Psychotherapy* is

long overdue. Kramer leads us on an insightful journey, cul-
minating in a superb final chapter. Readers will find themselves easily identifying with many of the issues presented,
agreeing and, at times, disagreeing, but always realizing that
the discussion has profound implications. Kramer's own
carefully conducted clinical research supports his arguments
convincingly.

Kramer approaches psychodynamic psychotherapy from
its broadest perspective. He is not wedded to an individual
school but recognizes the intricacy of systems that explore the
deepest roots of personality. He thoughtfully integrates a number of related but not often discussed themes in psychotherapy. For example, he takes the position that psychotherapists
should discuss treatment goals with clients at the beginning
of treatment. At the same time, he recognizes that the goals of
treatment frequently change and that the aspirations proposed
at the beginning of psychotherapy are not necessarily those
realized at its end.

A major thesis of this book is that therapy is a process
that has a conclusion. Kramer does not believe in using a
list of criteria to determine when termination should occur;
ideally, it should be initiated by the client and genuinely supported by the practitioner. Throughout the book, Kramer
unveils his own ideas about termination and offers concise
explanations of the theoretical underpinnings of his stance.

The question of who initiates the ending of psychotherapy is multifaceted. For the client, the therapy experience
of acceptance as a special individual is often unique and
extremely intense. If the client has not been able to effect
such acceptance in a relationship outside psychotherapy, it
can be difficult for him or her to give up the treatment experience. It is sometimes necessary for a client to end treatment
in order to achieve the level of intimacy desired outside the
treatment situation.

At the same time, the psychotherapist's own characteristics may complicate ending a client's treatment. For example, a therapist may not want an individual to end his or her
sessions because some goals are yet to be achieved. The thera-

pist may feel less than successful if the treatment ends before all objectives have been met. Simultaneously, the sheer enjoyment of helping an individual blossom may be so rewarding that it is difficult for the therapist to end this gratification. This may be especially true if the treatment process with a particular client has become enjoyable and the psychotherapist envisions working with the next client as more problematic and demanding and less gratifying. In addition, therapists may unconsciously resist terminating their treatment of clients who provide much gratification if the therapists' personal lives are empty or conflicted.

A precise, complicated, and honest approach to psychotherapy that regards a client's health as well as her or his potential and desire for a fuller life is beautifully modeled in *Positive Endings in Psychotherapy*. The thesis that a client matures through the therapeutic process is a consistent theme. Psychotherapists overly obsessed with psychopathology and lacking enthusiasm for human potential will struggle with Kramer's dedication to letting clients determine the ending of their treatment. And some practitioners will be upset by his belief that the client's wishes should be honored when client and psychotherapist truly disagree on whether termination is appropriate. However, if the reader accepts his premise of client growth and self-determination, his logic is difficult to fault.

The field of psychodynamic psychotherapy owes a true debt to Steven Aaron Kramer. His research and theory will lead practitioners to reflect more thoughtfully and complexly on the termination of psychotherapy with clients. We are fortunate to have someone so concisely address this intricate and not often explored aspect of psychotherapy. We also benefit from Kramer's personal candor and excellent writing style.

June 1990   Edward P. Sheridan
Professor and Chairman
Division of Psychology
Northwestern University Medical School

In memory of my father, Gus Kramer (affectionately known as Babe). A man of few words but many deeds, he taught me the importance of treating others with respect and dignity.

This book is also dedicated to the hope that the professions of psychology, social work, and psychiatry may channel more of their energies, not into professional and personal power struggles, but rather into the synthesis and integration of creative treatment strategies. There is more that binds us together than keeps us apart.

Preface

The progress a patient makes during therapy should be enriched and heightened by a positive treatment ending. When termination issues are ignored or mishandled, the whole of therapy is jeopardized. This crucial ending phase remains, however, largely uncharted territory, the neglected and ill-defined chapter of every treatment experience. Guidelines for conducting this part of psychotherapy are virtually nonexistent. There is a lack of consensus with regard to every aspect of termination, including the role of therapist and patient, criteria for ending, and strategies according to patient diagnosis. Although the beginning and middle stages of open-ended psychotherapy are generally well documented, the termination phase has not been fully investigated. In addition, there are virtually no theoretical and practical guidelines for clinicians to follow as they work through endings with their patients.

Terminating a psychotherapeutic relationship can be as difficult, or even more difficult, than ending any other relationship. However, the intricacies of a clinician-client relationship add to the complexities of closure and make it unique from life's other endings. Saying goodbye to a lover or a dying relative are subjects that have been well explored in recent years. But saying goodbye to a valued client or therapist has not been examined as deeply or as usefully. This is particularly true of the transference and countertransference issues that often play a negative role in psychotherapeutic endings.

The purpose of this work is to help psychotherapists better understand the termination process in order to conduct it with the confidence and comfort that lead to positive treatment endings. It is mainly written for practitioners of open-ended, long-term, individual psychotherapy; however, those who practice within time limits, contracts, or agency constraints also will find valuable information here. The primary audience includes psychologists, clinical social workers, and psychiatrists with a variety of orientations such as ego psychology, Jungian theory, classical analytic theory, client-centered approaches, and existential theory, to name but a few. The book is also directed to those who practice a combination of these approaches. This variety of mental health clinicians, plus the increasing number of psychotherapy consumers, underlines the need for understanding and improving the termination phase.

The observations and guidelines presented in this book are based partially on the data and results of my 1982 and 1986 studies of the termination process in open-ended individual psychotherapy in private practice settings (Kramer, 1986; see the Resource for details). This work is also founded on my clinical observations during sixteen years of open-ended, long-term psychotherapy with hundreds of people in both private practice and community mental health centers, as well as my decade of supervisory experience.

My style as a psychotherapist has been influenced strongly by both the classical analytic and humanistic schools. The humanistic approaches first attracted me to psychotherapy; I found myself quite skeptical of the classical psychodynamic treatment and theory that was predominant in my professional education. This skepticism was reinforced by the culture of my first position at a grass roots community mental health center. My second position, however, immersed me in the traditional psychoanalytic thinking of a teaching institution. The dichotomy of these two settings encouraged me to further explore and question the theories of psychotherapy.

It was Heinz Kohut's self psychology approach and his unique understanding and use of empathy that drew me closer to my present practice of therapy. Like all skeptics, however, I do not agree with all self psychology theories, especially as they pertain to once- or twice-weekly psychotherapy. I also find myself very much in tune with the work of Carl Rogers and with the client-centered perspective, again particularly regarding the issue of empathy and respect for the client's autonomy.

Therefore, this book is written from both the humanistic and psychodynamic perspectives, despite the fact that I am at times critical of the psychoanalytic approach. The integration of selected humanistic tenets and psychodynamic ones is important to me. I do not believe they are mutually exclusive as theories or in clinical practice. Although my bias is clear, the intent of this book is not to encourage practitioners to change their theoretical orientations or clinical styles. Rather, it is to enable psychotherapists to make the entire treatment experience a better one for their clients and themselves through clearer understanding of the complexities of the termination process.

In the first chapter I discuss whether the goal of treatment is change or cure, and compare the views of five major theorists—Freud, Kohut, Jung, Rank, and Rogers—on this subject. The beginning, middle, and final stages of therapy are described, with emphasis on the idea that the seeds of the ending are sown at the start. Also presented are therapists' views of the ideal termination.

Chapter Two focuses on practitioner and patient roles in commencing the end of therapy and presents case studies illustrating both possibilities. Positive and negative terminations are discussed in depth.

Chapter Three presents a variety of criteria for ending therapy that are drawn from the literature, including case studies, as well as observations from my own research. Examples and interviews with practitioners focus on how such criteria are actually employed. The value of using criteria is analyzed, including their relevancy and potential for harm in the termination context.

In Chapter Four, passages from Judith Rossner's novel *August* are used to illustrate two contrasting terminations with a patient suffering from severe character disorder. The emphasis is on working with extremely fragile clients and the special issues that can arise around termination of treatment. I conclude with a positive model applicable to almost all treatment endings but most salient when the client is vulnerable due to earlier developmental losses or other repeated self-injuries.

The special and useful perspective of patients who are therapists are examined in Chapter Five. This chapter presents personal treatment experiences of practitioners and analyzes subjects such as who initiated termination and what criteria were applied. A number of clinicians offer their own ending experiences, and a verbatim interview with a therapist patient illuminates some of the issues.

Nontherapist clients' views of terminations are the focus of Chapter Six. Two in-depth interviews describe a positive and a negative treatment ending, and the sensitive matter of handling fees is discussed as it relates to termination.

Chapter Seven examines what transpires in the last hours of therapy, with special attention to abrupt terminations and vanishing patients. An annotated transcript of a final session is presented as a step-by-step description of a positive treatment denouement.

Chapter Eight offers guidelines adaptable to various theoretical approaches for helping therapists structure positive terminations. It ends with a final case illustration and suggestions for future research.

Every treatment has a finish—this universality alone should encourage practitioners to examine, reflect on, and strive to improve the content and process of the psychotherapeutic ending so that it may become not only an ending, but a new beginning. The final phase of treatment is the most uncomfortable for both patients and practitioners. It is also the least understood and complex of all aspects of psychotherapy. The purpose of this book is to illuminate the process and, by so doing, help therapists reach more meaningful and positive endings.

Chicago, Illinois   Steven Aaron Kramer
June 1990

Acknowledgments

First I must thank the two most important people in my life, my wife, Jane Elizabeth, and my son, Sean Zachary, for their patience while I was working on this manuscript. Truly, I am blessed to have them in my life.

A special thanks to Mary Sheehy, who usually managed to decipher my hieroglyphics. Her diligence and dependability were a great help from the inception of the book through its completion.

Sanna Hans-Longden's help in preparing this manuscript was invaluable. Her grasp of ideas and concepts in areas in which she is not formally trained is amazing. She is truly a renaissance woman.

I would also like to thank Gracia A. Alkema, senior editor at Jossey-Bass, for her enthusiasm and support during the completion of this manuscript.

S.A.K.

The Author

Steven Aaron Kramer maintains a private practice in psychotherapy in Chicago, Illinois. He is an associate in the Depart-
ment of Psychiatry and Behavioral Sciences at Northwestern
University Medical School. He received both his B.A. degree
in psychology and his M.A. degree in community psychology
from Northeastern Illinois University with high honors. Kramer earned his Ph.D. degree at the University of Chicago.

Kramer is a member of the American Psychological
Association and the National Association of Social Workers.
Related to the subject matter of this book is his article on the
termination process in open-ended psychotherapy, which
appeared in *Psychotherapy: Theory Research and Practice* in
1986. His major interest is the synthesis and integration of
various theoretical approaches in the treatment of disorders
of the self, specifically eating disorders.

Positive Endings
in Psychotherapy

1

Preparing for Positive Endings:
The End Begins at the Beginning

If termination of psychotherapy is handled with the care and consideration it demands, it can be a positive and productive experience. The following statement illustrates such an experience from the client's point of view.

> My termination was a good one. I was one of the lucky ones. I know a lot of people who've had bad experiences. In my circumstance, there was a very good relationship and rapport. It felt mutual. It's interesting that it is difficult to remember who initiated it—it just felt right. I assume it was me. We were tuned in together. Ending was dealt with by my therapist as a process. You just don't terminate. We talked about grief, future problems that might arise, and lots more. I did not feel pushed out, but very supported—that it was time and I would be fine. My desire to end was treated by my therapist as a positive choice. The tools I had learned in therapy I was now able to carry over to other situations.

Note: Unless attributed otherwise, all quotations, case studies, and vignettes are drawn from my own research.

1

However, ending this unique relationship can be difficult for both therapist and patient because whoever expresses the immediate feeling that it is time to stop frequently meets great resistance.

I had been feeling that things were at a standstill for a long time. I went into therapy because I didn't feel very good about myself. So when I didn't feel better, I automatically thought it was my fault. Twice I said something like, "I still am not feeling very good." My therapist said, "It takes time." This time I got my courage up and said, "I don't think I am making much progress." I was not sure I wanted to stop but I thought she should know how frustrated I was.

Well, before I knew, the therapist was attacking me. She said the reason I was not doing well was because I was distancing myself from her and that was my major problem. That's why she said I didn't have many friends and why I could not form a lasting relationship with a man. Then she brought up stopping therapy. She said it would be a good idea because I could not get close enough to her to get better.

I felt betrayed and abused. If she really thought all this, why did she continue to see me for over a year?

More than any other phase of the treatment process, the ending calls upon therapists to examine and understand their own needs and feelings. It is a time to look deeply inside and honestly confront one's dependence, anxieties, and fears, whether they be emotional or economic. Many practitioners feel the same as a nationally renowned therapist whose response to one of my research questions was "I am uncomfortable about termination and cannot articulate adequately on the subject. I would be glad to talk to you about diagnosis or other treatment issues."

Endings are so inextricably tied to the basic human connection—the bond between parent and child—that fears of abandonment and rejection can be stirred up in both patient and therapist. If great care is not taken in the termination phase, early developmental pain may be reexperienced and reinforced, with devastating effects on the entire treatment process.

The manner in which a therapist structures a treatment, usually determined by his or her theoretical base and individual style, may be of major importance for that person's understanding of the termination process. A general philosophy that is respectful of patients and sees them as autonomous, proactive, and self-directive is essential if the therapist is to facilitate healthy, productive endings. The abilities to be empathic, tolerant, and nonmanipulative are crucial. Many of the teachings of the self-psychology school and the client-centered approach exemplify this philosophy. In their similarities as well as in their differences, these approaches support and enhance the client growth and self-development that are so important to positive terminations.*

Is the Goal Change or Cure?

A discussion of the termination process must address the question of whether emotional conflict, mental illness, or psychopathology can be "cured." Theories of what constitutes normality also are linked to the concept of cure. Gaskill (1980) reports on periodic symposia that have assessed therapeutic objectives and comments, "These evaluations reflect considerable divergence of opinion as to the extent and depth of the changes expected while maintaining the achievement of a satisfactory termination" (p. 10). While the divergence of opinion is certainly true, the "satisfactory termination" Gaskill mentions seems to be the therapist's and not the patient's. He adds, "In reviewing these assessments, one is immediately struck by the trend towards more modest expectations with

---

*I will employ the terms "patient" and "client" interchangeably because neither term satisfactorily describes the therapeutic relationship and because I wish to remain theoretically neutral on this point.

less emphasis on 'cure' and less assurance of the permanence of change" (p. 10).

In my opinion, if there is such a trend, it has not filtered down to most practicing psychodynamic clinicians. The idealization of classical analysis with its perfectionistic, idiosyncratic, and frequently lofty goals is still very prevalent. Even if there were a strong movement away from the idea of cure, a skeptic could easily ask why it has taken a century for Freud's most loyal followers to adhere to his basic tenet that moderate goals in analysis and psychotherapy are essential. This is a crucial concept, especially as it relates to understanding the termination process and formulating guidelines for it.

Practitioners who believe that psychogenic or emotional disturbances are analogous to some physical anomalies and that they can be totally restored to "normalcy" (Kernberg, 1977; Masterman, 1976) may base their termination criteria on the concept of cure, meaning total alleviation of all conflicts and presenting problems. However, it is somewhat grandiose, or at least overly ambitious and unrealistic, to expect a total cure of a patient's psychopathology. Aiming for such an unobtainable goal often leaves both patient and practitioner with feelings of failure. Supporting this view is Jung, who writes: "There is widespread prejudice that analysis is something like a 'cure' to which one submits for a time and is then discharged healed. . . . That is a layman's error left over from the early days of psychoanalysis" (1966 [1916], p. 72). Rank (1945) is also opposed to the belief that cure is feasible or even desirable: "The therapist ought to know, and share his knowledge with the patient, that there is no criterion for 'cure' in psychotherapy, yes perhaps no 'cures' in the medical sense in terms of the removal of a disturbing cause" (p. 190). At the other end on the spectrum are therapists who look solely to symptom alleviation as a yardstick of change. These include theorists whose viewpoints are behavioral (Gambrill, 1978), task-centered (Reid and Epstein, 1972), and problem-solving (Haley, 1976).

Those therapeutic disciplines that work with specific

and identifiable symptoms, contractual agreements, or predetermined time limits do not have the same confusion as the
open-ended psychotherapies about how and when to stop
treatment. They may have the opposite problem: when to
continue. One important lesson to be learned from short-
term, behavioral, problem-solving, or task-centered therapists
is their adherence to obtainable goals. While open-ended clinicians cannot, and probably should not, be as unidimen-
sional as the former groups, their treatments and terminations
might be more satisfying for themselves and their clients if
they cleave a bit more to achieving agreed-upon goals.

Whether a practitioner is a supporter of total cure
or partial modification, his or her theoretical perspective,
especially regarding the etiology of psychopathology, is an
essential factor in the decision to end treatment and in the
determination of criteria for termination. Jahoda (1958)
reviews a wide range of criteria that have been suggested
for defining "positive mental health." Most of those for
"normality" have to do with insight into one's self, as
shown by self-actualization, investment in living, accepting
one's limitations and potentials, and awareness of one's
basic motivations. Thus, mentally healthy persons develop
a "rich, differential life," participating in "various pursuits
not restricted to what must be done for sheer survival"
(pp. 22–35). Among other primary criteria for positive mental health are accurate perceptions of reality, self-direction
or autonomy, and the ability to resist stress or anxiety.
Those with a more behavioral orientation believe that
understanding and being able to describe one's actions,
motivations, and behavior are often not adequate in helping people change. It has been demonstrated that many
individuals have profound insight into their problems, but
fail to be able to move beyond the constrictions of their
psychopathology.

I believe that change, or growth, is a more appropriate
concept for expressing desirable therapeutic outcomes than is
cure. If therapists adhere to a model of change and growth,
they are less likely to strive for unobtainable goals and perfec-

tionistic treatment outcomes. Diverse views on how to end psychotherapy, however, must not prevent a deeper understanding of the final phase or the establishment of practical criteria for determining the optimal termination of treatment. (Chapter Four presents an in-depth discussion of such criteria.)

Theories of Change and Cure

A brief survey of five contrasting theoreticians who have had great influence on psychotherapeutic theory and practice provides some background for better understanding cure, change, and normalcy, as these concepts relate to the whole ending process, including the initiation of termination and the criteria for it. In spite of their major contributions, however, these theoreticians, and almost all the others, have written less about the ending stage than about other aspects of treatment.

Included here are Sigmund Freud, with his tremendous impact on psychotherapy and personality theory; Heinz Kohut, who represents a contemporary analytic viewpoint that differs fairly radically from the orthodox Freudian school; Carl Gustav Jung, with his unique and disparate ideas regarding human nature, treatment, and termination; Otto Rank, whose original theories of time and termination have heavily influenced the professions of humanistic psychology and social work; and Carl Rogers, a humanistic/phenomenological psychologist who was one of the forerunners of self psychology.

Freud. The theory of instinctual drives is central to classical Freudian thought, although changes have occurred from its original concept to present-day interpretations. Freud's position shifted over the years, with his emphasis evolving from an almost exclusive id psychology to a greater recognition and acknowledgment of the role of the ego. It can be postulated that the transitions Freud made within instinctual theory influenced his conception of cure and his views on termination.

The ending of psychoanalytic treatment must come when the analytic work is finished. To Freud, the task is complete with the resolution of the Oedipal complex, which indicates that the patient has more control over instinctual drives. Berenstein (1987, p. 26) reminds us that Freud believed "analytic therapy resolves current conflicts only" and thus treatment is not aimed at "preventing future instinctual conflicts."

Discussing the strength of the instincts and the feasibility of a total cure, Freud (1963) wrote, "A permanent settlement of an instinctual demand [is] as a rule impossible and not even desirable. . . . A change does occur but it is often partial" (p. 242). It would appear that modern Freudian theorists have essentially ignored this shift from total cure to partial change, which may account in part for the prolonged nature of individual psychoanalysis today.

In Freud's later years, he appeared to look realistically at the concept of cure as well as at other outcome expectations of psychoanalysis. Blum (1987), critiquing Freud's classic article "Analysis: Terminable and Interminable" writes, "The realistic appraisal of the limits of analysis would be swept aside in the later idealization of analysis and its popular appeal in the 1950s. Analysts had to be confronted with and reminded of the limitations of analyzability, suitability, termination, and outcome" (p. 38). From id to ego to self-deficit, analytic theory has changed in some ways. Practicing clinicians, however, seem reluctant and slow in applying new theories, especially as they relate to termination.

Kohut. Heinz Kohut, a former classical Freudian analyst and perhaps the most brilliant and humanistic of all psychodynamic theoreticians, proposed a framework called "a psychology of the self" (1977, pp. 249–267). While Freud based his theories on a conflict model, Kohut focused on a deficit model. The emergence of the self, according to Kohut, should be viewed as a developmental process that ranges from distinct physical sensations through a subjective feeling of uniqueness to a strong sense of differentiation and separate identity. He postulated that the self is composed of two different parts, the grandiose self and the idealized parental imago.

The grandiose self is the budding, original feeling of grandness and infallibility. As a person matures, the grandiose self is responsible for the emergence of a sense of pride and self-worth. The idealized parental imago provides the child with an adult to project the feeling of omnipotence and perfection. The self structure either develops in a healthy manner or in a pathological one, depending greatly on the self-object's (caretaker's) ability to respond empathetically to the child's blossoming self.

Kohut (1977) felt termination of treatment should take place "when we have completed one or the other of two specific tasks: (1) When after the analytic penetration of the defensive structures, the *primary defect* in the self has been exposed and, via working through and transmuting internalization, sufficiently filled out so that the formerly defective structures of the self have now become functionally reliable; (2) we have also reached the termination phase in the analysis of a narcissistic personality disorder when—after the patient has achieved cognitive and affective mastery with regard to the defenses surrounding the primary defect in the self, with regard to the relationship between these—the *compensatory structures* have now become functionally reliable, independent of the area in which this success was achieved" (1977, p. 4).

Because of differences in theoretical frameworks between Freud and Kohut, especially in etiology of psychopathology, their ideas of what constitutes successful treatment and intrapsychic criteria for termination are radically different. Upon close examination, however, there are commonalities in the external, general manifestations observed when these sets of criteria are met. For example, Freud (1957) discusses a patient's recovery in terms of "whether the subject is left with a sufficient amount of capacity for enjoyment and of efficiency" (vol. 16, p. 457), and a major criterion of success for Kohut, as well as others, is that the patient has been helped to love and work more efficaciously.

If our goals and expectations are too high, most open-ended psychotherapies will be labeled as "premature terminations," thus reinforcing the continuing cycle of perfectionistic aspirations, premature endings, and feelings of failure for both clinicians and patients. I am not suggesting that we strive for low standards, only realistic ones: If therapists are taught that anything short of perfect outcome is a failure, they can easily feel pressured to hold on to patients until they are "cured."

Jung. C. G. Jung appears to have had a unique view of personality before he participated in the Freudian "inner circle." His humanistic theories are directly related to a conceptualization of treatment that encourages positive endings.

To Jung, psychopathology results when an individual's capacities are thwarted and not allowed to develop positively. Thus, the paramount goal in analytic psychotherapy is to help the patient's creative potentialities flourish. This growth takes place by helping the patient become aware of and in touch with his or her personal and nonpersonal (collective) unconscious. Treatment evolves from a focus on the patient's conscious perceptions, thoughts, feelings, attitudes, and values, to an exploration of the personal and collective unconscious. Although for both Freud and Jung dreams are the "royal road to the unconscious," Jung believed that ultimate understanding came through the collective unconscious: "In addition to our immediate consciousness, which is of a thoroughly personal nature and which we believe to be the only empirical psyche (even if we tack on the personal unconscious as an appendix), there exists a second psychic system of a collective, universal, and impersonal nature which is identical in all individuals. . . . It consists of pre-existent forms, the archetypes, which can only become conscious secondarily and which give definite form to certain psychic contents" (1959, p. 43).

In contrast to Freud's more rigid and inflexible system, with its narrow, pessimistic view of human nature and psychopathology, Jung's system is open, flexible, focused on the growth of the self, and almost mystical. Like most of Jung's techniques, termination is to be individualized, based on the patient's needs. However, he does suggest the following circumstances under which treatment may end:

(1) After receiving a piece of good advice; (2) After making a fairly complete but nevertheless adequate confession; (3) After having recognized some hitherto unconscious but psychic content whose realization gives a new impetus to one's life and activity; (4) After a hard-won separation from the childhood psyche; (5) After having worked out a new and rational mode of adaptation to perhaps difficult or unusual circumstances and surroundings; (6) After the disappearance of painful symptoms; (7) After some positive turn of fortune such as an examination, engagement, marriage, divorce, change of profession, etc.; (8) After having found one's way back to the church or creed to which one previously belonged, or after a conversion; (9) After having begun to build up a practical philosophy of life (a "philosophy" in the classical sense of the word) [1953 (1944), p. 4].

Jung's final point illuminates the importance of a fundamental principle in analytical therapy: the individuation process, the striving toward self-actualization and growth. Clearly, to Jung, entrance into this process is the optimal reason or circumstance under which termination should take place.

A marked difference can be seen between the orthodox Freudian method of terminating and the termination prototype used by Jung and his followers. The Freudians would adhere to the principle of meeting on a regular basis until the very end of treatment. In contrast, the Jungian theorists would introduce early in treatment a flexible and variable session schedule. As Jung writes: "I content myself with a maximum of four consultations a week. With the beginning of synthetic treatment it is of advantage to spread out the consultations. I then generally reduce them to one or two hours a week, for the patient must learn to go on his way" (1954 [1935], p. 20). Rather than encourage dependency and regression, Jung suggests from the onset of treatment an adaptation to the environmental realities of life. He further states, "I break off the treatment every ten weeks or so in order to throw him back on his normal milieu. In this way he is not alienated from his world for he really suffers from his tendency to live at another's expense" (1954 [1935], pp. 26–27).

Rank. Otto Rank, like most psychoanalysts of his time, was a close associate and friend of Freud. The rift in their relationship widened when Rank published his article and eventual book, *The Trauma of Birth* (1952). His departure from Freud's theories is very relevant to a discussion and understanding of the termination process.

Rank believed that all anxiety can be traced to the traumatic experience of birth—the fright of emerging from the womb into the external environment. To alleviate the effects of this trauma, he endeavored to shock the patient by imposing an ending date for the analysis. Thus Rank believed not only in the primacy of the birth trauma and the relationship of the child to both mother and father, but also that the original birth trauma had to be brought into the present and lived out emotionally. It is the projection or transference of the mother onto the analyst and the subsequent second or less traumatic "birth" or separation that are crucial.

The use of time limits, determined at some point in treatment, is essential to Rankian treatment. Taft writes, "The end setting for Rank is not just a means for shortening analysis or an announcement of cure, but the most therapeutic instrument available for treatment of the neurosis" (1966, p. 78).

In an even more heretical act, Rank drastically altered his conceptualization of the ego, which is clearly relevant to discussion of termination. The ego was renamed the "will," which to Rank was a central psychological principle, a "positive guiding organization and integration of self which utilizes creatively, as well as inhibits and controls the instinctual drives" (1945, p. 112). As opposed to the traditional, reductionistic view of termination—with its emphasis on resistance, transference, and acting out—Rank's concept (similar to that of Jung) is proactive, striving toward autonomous functioning and self-direction.

Rogers. The research of Carl A. Rogers, which culminated in the development of client-centered therapy, began with his first publication in 1942, "Newer Concepts in Practice," in *Counseling and Psychotherapy.* Rogers received traditional psychoanalytic training but was more affected by the humanistically oriented theories of Otto Rank than by the Freudian postulates. Like many psychotherapeutic theorists, Rogers did not write a great deal about termination. However, his respect for self-direction of clients and his unique use of empathy make his work extremely important for understanding the termination process. His theories and philosophies are used throughout this book to help structure positive endings.

Client-centered therapy is based on a phenomenological theory of personality development that says to understand human beings and to conceptualize a viable treatment structure, the practitioner must focus on the individual's subjective experiences, thoughts, and feelings. In contrast to the Freudian emphasis on recapitulation of the past and the behaviorist emphasis on past and current conditioning, Rogers believed that human functioning and the process of growth can best be understood by exploring the human being's subjective perceptions in the here and now: "The best vantage point for understanding behavior is from the internal frame of reference of the individual himself" (1951, p. 494). Thus, Rogers was one of the forerunners of self psychology.

Freud and Rogers each developed their theories from direct work with patients. True to his humanistic underpinnings, Rogers believed that the nature of human beings is positive, proactive, and self-directing. The client-centered approach proposes a set of core conditions that need to be present if therapeutic change is to occur. A basic tenet and perhaps a precursor to all later conditions is that the client and therapist need to be in psychological contact. This relationship is the essence of therapeutic change to Rogers. The client experiences some subjective vulnerability or "incongruence"; thus, there is a rift between this experience and his or her self-concept. To be effective in the therapeutic relationship, the practitioner needs to feel and display warmth, genuineness, and humanity, remaining as nonjudgmental as possible. This "unconditional positive regard" is crucial if the client is to flourish and grow as well as explore deeper levels of self. The integration of newly found or newly experienced feelings with a different, improved self-concept results in the emergence of a healthier, integrated sense of self.

Through empathic understanding, the therapist joins the client in this subjective experience and offers a unique grasp or comprehension that is in itself healing. Through verbalization and attitude, the therapist does everything possible to convey his or her understanding of the client's perceptions and feelings.

In his classic work, "On Becoming a Person" (1961), Rogers conceptualizes the change process as seven stages. These stages, he suggests, should be examined on a continuum, so that "whether one demonstrated three stages or fifty, there would still be all the intermediate points" (p. 131). The seventh and final stage is the most pertinent for the elucidation of the termination process as it relates to client-centered psychotherapy. According to Rogers, "the client often seems to go on into the seventh and final stage without much need of the therapist's help" (p. 151).

In effect, what Rogers describes in his stages of therapy is his optimal definition of the "fully functioning person." These characteristics can be viewed as termination criteria or the ideal transformation of a human being's self: "The client has now incorporated the quality of motion, of flow, of changingness, into every aspect of his psychological life, and this becomes its outstanding characteristic. . . . He perceives himself as responsibly related to his problems. Indeed, he feels a fully responsible relationship to his life in all its fluid aspects. He lives fully in himself as a constantly changing flow of process" (p. 155).

From Rogers's own words, certain assumptions can be made regarding termination. The name of the entire approach to treatment, client-centered, leaves no doubt that it is the client who charts the course of therapy, including when it should end. The therapist following this approach is con-

stantly empathically connected to the client and so understands, often before the client does, that termination cues are
occurring. Although the therapist would never initiate termination, he or she could reflect these out-of-awareness feelings,
thus beginning the process. Because process and fluidity are
paramount to the client-centered theoretical approach, the
idea of a fixed state of health or cure runs counter to this
perspective of treatment. Rogers's stages of therapy constitute
a process continuum: "A client might start therapy at about
stage two and end about stage four with both client and therapist being quite legitimately satisfied that substantial progress had been made. It would occur very rarely, if ever, that a
client who fully exemplified stage one would move to a point
where he fully exemplified stage seven" (p. 127).

The Ending Originates in the Beginning

Rogers's seven stages of treatment can also be viewed as three
general ones—the beginning, middle, and final stages. He
and the other major theorists discussed earlier understood that
the groundwork for the treatment goal—whether it be cure,
change, or normalcy—must be established at the start. Negative therapeutic endings almost always originate in the beginning and middle phases of treatment; they do not suddenly
occur as the relationship is coming to closure. These stages
do not proceed in a linear progression, but are, like a spiral,
inextricably connected. For the purposes of discussion, however, we will separate the three components to see how they
are linked.

Beginning Stage. The work of the beginning stage should
include establishment of the therapeutic alliance between practitioner and patient, diagnosis or assessment of the patient's
presenting problems, education of the patient about the treatment process itself, and the start of a mutual collaboration
between client and clinician.

Establishing a bond or working rapport at the start is
vital to all that follows in the treatment relationship. According to Rogers's client-centered philosophy (1961), "The task

of psychotherapy is to help the person achieve, through a special relationship with a therapist, good communication within himself. Once this is achieved, he can communicate more freely and more effectively with others" (p. 330). Gittelson (1962), a classical analyst who also believes that curative elements of treatment start in the first phase, underscores the personal relationship between patient and therapist. However, he proposes a more directive posture during the beginning phase that encourages the therapist to advise, recommend, and guide; he believes the patient develops autonomy as treatment progresses.

The essential objective, no matter how it is conceptualized, is to form a relationship with the client that promotes self-directiveness and personal growth. If a positive alliance is not formed at the start of psychotherapy, less positive outcomes and certainly fewer growthful endings will occur.

The diagnostic/assessment aspect of the beginning stage can be approached in terms of a formal diagnostic format or in a slower, more evolutionary manner. The diagnostic technique uses a designated number of sessions to gather information through structured interviews and standardized tests leading to a specific treatment diagnosis. In the slower, evolutionary, process-oriented assessment, clients act out their issues on the therapeutic stage, demonstrating in a naturally occurring way their personality structures, intrapsychic conflicts, and quality of relationships. The practitioner asks questions to clarify and reflect, not to direct the sessions. However, whether a therapist uses one of these approaches or both, premature diagnosis should not take precedence over a natural and open-ended building of the treatment relationship.

One practitioner, for example, who uses a more formal diagnostic procedure, tells new clients that he will designate two to six sessions to assess their needs. He uses psychological tests and in-depth interviews, separately or together. Another therapist conducts the assessment phase strictly according to process. She evaluates clients by examining transference and countertransference issues while observing each nuance: Some clients may come late to the first few sessions or may have trouble leaving; others might have immediate and intense feelings about the practitioner or report dreams. Therapists may use one or both of these diagnostic/assessment techniques.

A frequently neglected step in the beginning of treatment is educating the patient about the therapeutic process, including its ending. This educational stage should include some discussion about length of treatment, goals of therapy, and mutual expectations. Fromm-Reichman, in her classic work *Principles of Intensive Psychotherapy,* writes: "The explanation of the psychotherapeutic process should be followed by a short discussion of expectations about the outcome of the treatment" (1950, p. 62). Practitioners can give patients an approximate idea of how long their treatments might last, drawing on their own clinical backgrounds and current research. A thirty-two-year-old professional woman, who sought therapy because she was feeling extremely anxious and insecure, was told by her seasoned, analytically trained therapist that he felt the approximate treatment length would be eighteen months to two years. This was clearly conveyed in an early session. As a result, the patient relaxed and entered into the work more easily, believing that her problems could be handled and knowing that the treatment would have an end.

Such discussions also might lead to the idea of different levels of treatment. Eleanor M. was totally overwhelmed and close to being hospitalized when she first entered treatment with Dr. Rosalie W. The precipitant was her increasingly intimate relationship with a man. The relationship seemed headed toward marriage, which stirred up distress over years of incest perpetrated upon her by her father. Owing to the patient's severe crisis state, Dr. W.'s first task was to enable Ms. M. to regain her psychological equilibrium. As they were progressing toward this goal, a second goal emerged: to not only regain her premorbid levels of functioning but also to learn to feel even better—to develop a more cohesive self structure. The patient could have decided to work through only the first layer of treatment, stopping when she achieved the first goal. However, she opted to continue. Such a choice of levels of therapeutic intervention ought to be discussed in the first sessions to avoid later misunderstandings about when the treatment should be finished. Unfortunately, too few therapists bring up these subjects at the commencement of treatment.

The core concepts of time, goals, and patient edification must be addressed in the beginning phase of therapy in order to create a mutual collaboration between clinician and client. Involving the patient at the onset of treatment is crucial if a smooth and positive termination has any chance to evolve. This collaboration reinforces the patient's autonomy and steadily encourages the emergence of a more cohesive self structure. If, instead, all the guidelines and issues are determined by the therapist, the patient becomes infantilized and the practitioner retains the responsibility for the entire process of change and, ultimately, termination. To avoid this all too frequent kind of occurrence, practitioner and client must resolve, in the early stages of psychotherapy, the conflict between idealistic, grandiose, perfectionistic goals and obtainable, realistic ones. This is where the discord originates that may later lead to both patient and therapist striving for the impossible so as to avoid or postpone termination, consciously or unconsciously.

Middle Stage. The middle phase can be described as the working or substantive stage. It is during this period that the seeds for either positive or negative terminations that were planted in the beginning continue to develop and grow.

Like the beginning, the middle can be defined by the clinician's theoretical orientation. In Blanck and Blanck's (1974) ego psychology approach, a modified form of classical analysis, "the middle phase ensues when the transference manifestations are evident, when an ongoing working alliance is established and when motivation is assured" (p. 149). In Rogers's (1961) client-centered philosophy, the substance of the middle phase is to listen with a profound understanding in order to capture the essence of a client's communication. Self-psychologists such as Kohut advocate that patients' goals are not obtained by resolving conflicting drives, but by building structure via empathy and interpretation. While Kohut (1984) does not speak of beginning, middle, and ending stages, he does differentiate between the understanding phase and the explaining phase, which though interwoven and mutually dependent can be separately discerned.

The development of terminations that result in unsatisfying partings for both patient and therapist can occur in an insidious fashion. During the middle stage, it becomes easy to lose sight of the presenting problems, goals, and reasons for the commencement of the therapy. It is important that the patient's progress be discussed throughout the course of psychotherapy. For example, the analytically trained therapist mentioned above who commendably discussed length of treatment and goals at the start, sad to say, never mentioned the subject again. This lack of follow-through subsequently became an obstacle in the course of that particular treatment relationship, especially in regard to the ending.

The difference between perfectionistic and realistic goals is of the utmost importance here. During the middle stage, especially in protracted treatment, therapists can go wrong in one of two ways: They can see change where little has occurred or they can fail to see change that has taken place. Both situations have negative implications for the termination process. Especially in open-ended psychodynamic psychotherapies, there is an ever-present temptation to "dig deeper," open up more issues, make more of the unconscious conscious, strive for more self-actualization and more insight. The model in its purest form encourages a perpetual process. Getting lost in the process, especially with a patient with whom the practitioner has become closely involved, can sabotage a good treatment experience. A thirty-five-year-old man who initially came into treatment to deal with chronic headaches found that within six to eight months, his headaches had ceased. The therapy, however, continued for thirteen more years and took on its own life. The fact that treatment went from dealing with a specific symptom to this endless process of self-exploration was never dealt with overtly by the therapist. Neither party knew how or when to end; the sessions might have gone on for another decade if the therapist had not moved out of the city.

At times, patients also may have unconscious needs to hold on to symptoms or retard growth. Eleanor M. was able to get married after about a year of treatment with Dr. Rosalie W., in spite of her near-psychotic state at the start. She was doing extremely well in all areas of her life. She initiated, and Dr. W. supported, a reduction in session frequency from twice weekly to once a week. Both agreed there was more work to be done, but the therapist was very affirming of her progress. However, after another year, Dr. W. wondered, "Why is she still coming?" In examining the interactive process, she decided that the client associated feeling good, sane, and whole with therapy. Perhaps Ms. M. was afraid that ending therapy would risk a regression into the way she had felt as a child and when she entered treatment—neglected and abandoned by self-objects. Dr. W. broached the subject, not as an interpretation, but as an idea to explore together.

Such exploration is appropriate middle-stage work and should not be left for the termination phase. By not falling into the time warp that may characterize long-term, open-ended treatment in the core stage (and before that, in the beginning), Dr. W. kept the communication channels open. This led to a successful termination after several months. Dr. W. did not initiate the ending, but she did continue in each stage of therapy to keep the barriers to termination at a minimum, especially those barriers within herself.

Ending Stage. The final stage of therapy is the culmination of all the work that has gone before. Perjorative termination experiences are more likely to occur when the issues are not dealt with in the beginning and middle stages.

There is general agreement among the various professional disciplines that the ending phase is critical (Goldberg, 1975; Levinson, 1977; Weigert, 1952). According to Schafer (1973), "It is during termination that unspoken promises, expectations, transferences, and resistances on the part of both

persons in the therapeutic relationship may come to light"
(p. 138); "The potential for every significant human emotion
resides in the termination situation" (p. 147).

Several authors stress the positive aspects of termination
(Krebs, 1972; Smalley, 1967). Kanzer (reported in Robbins,
1975) finds that "relief, joy, and a hunger for new experiences
for which money, time, and psychological preparedness are
now available . . . militate against the traumatic aspects" of
termination (p. 172). Buxbaum (1950) describes termination
as similar to "the finale of a musical movement which repeats
the leading motives of a piece" (p. 188).

Many authors discuss the difficulties inherent in the
last stage of therapy (Fox, Nelson, and Bolman, 1969; Kauff,
1977; Schiff, 1962). Epstein (1980) and others feel that termination is more difficult for practitioners than clients (p. 257).
In spite of the conflicting attitudes toward the final stage of
treatment, many therapists have clear personal perceptions of
the perfect ending as one that is satisfying both to their clients
and to themselves. As is true of most of life's ideals, however,
these perceptions do not always match reality. Following are
descriptions of perfect terminations by a number of surveyed
clinicians, whose goals for endings encompass many of the
themes discussed in this book.

"The key for me," says therapist A. T., "would be a
feeling on both our parts that there had been a tremendous
amount of gain made. The client would feel extremely good
about the therapy. But each person is so individual and
unique. My respect for and belief in that principle get in the
way of coming up with the ideal." One criterion for termination that therapist A. T. uses is "people feeling better about
their 'selves' and this being reflected in their behavior. They
would exhibit freedom of behavior, feelings, and a range of
emotional expression from joy to sadness." He also looks for
changes in the therapeutic relationship as a gauge of change
and growth. "Clients would fully acknowledge their relationship with me, expressing their feelings about me, especially
what I meant to them. The client would see me as a person
who remains interested in them beyond my professional role."

This therapist's ideal termination is in tune with his client-centered, humanistic orientation. His theoretical approach emphasizes the use of relationships in psychotherapy and, especially relative to termination, places great value on understanding that the therapeutic relationship has time limits and thus functions as a metaphor for life, death, and all endings.

Several object-relations therapists, those who focus on preverbal separations and other experiences as essential areas of conflict to work through, expressed their ending goals. Therapist F. K. says that in her ideal termination, "patients would gradually come to the realization that they did not need treatment anymore. They would put less importance on me and more importance on them. They would feel alive, valuable, and knowledgeable. We would have accomplished what we set out to do." Like most of the others interviewed, this therapist stresses a vision of a natural, gradual process initiated by the client as well as a mutuality. In the fantasy termination, there is no disagreement.

Therapist F. K. continues with her ideal ending: "I would prefer patients come in for sessions less often, taper off gradually. I would be there for them during that time if they wanted to call for an extra session occasionally, with me acting as a transitional object. I think the concept of transitional objects serves as a good model for termination."

Therapist W. J., another psychodynamically oriented clinician, states: "The patient's autonomy is of the utmost importance regarding termination. Ideally, the patient would initiate it, set the date, and my primary task as always would be to analyze material." He says that in his utopian end to psychotherapy, the patient would "relive all the previously experienced emotions in the treatment." The major criteria he would use are dreams and his own intuition. Further, therapist W. J. would offer people choices. "They could go through a termination phase that would last about two months or longer, or quit sooner if they choose to, or set a date as soon as termination was brought up and stick to it."

Consonant with other therapists' ideal endings, this cli-

nician stresses the patient leading the way. There is a contra-
diction, however, when he insists on respecting patients'
autonomy but still analyzing and interpreting the termination
material. When there is total agreement, of course, there is
little conflict. But with this approach, it may be impossible
to make analytic interpretations that will not end up manip-
ulating the patient and that will interfere with respecting the
patient's autonomous, self-regulatory strivings.

Therapist R. B., a psychoanalytically trained practitioner, comments: "Patients decide to terminate—that's the
way it should be. I don't usually think about termination
until the patient stops coming in or announces that he or she
might not continue." This clinician is one of many therapists
who do not theorize about termination and have no plan for
working out an ending with a client.

Therapist M. H. calls himself an eclectic therapist
because he "takes the best from Gestalt and transactional
analysis theory, but also uses family systems, paradox, and
psychoanalytic concepts, especially transference and countertransference." He was quite candid during the research interview and disclosed some of his feelings about economic
concerns and how they relate to termination complexities and
countertransference issues. "Even though my practice is busy
and successful, it still scares me at times when clients are
going to leave. It is a time when I must deal with my own
self-interest, narcissistic issues, and do the best I can to work
through these feelings to be a better therapist. I believe that
people are kept in treatment too long because of these types
of issues."

This clinician integrates various psychotherapeutic theories in his ideal ending. "The client would initiate the termination and it would be mutually agreed upon. We would
take at least four to eight sessions that would focus on ending
and a final date would be set. Also, we would look at past
separations and losses and the connection to the psychotherapy termination. The client would mourn, but I would feel
sad, also. There would be some tears, some joy, and maybe
some touching. We would review the progress and growth

together. Finally, we would be able to say that we care a great deal for each other and the client would acknowledge that the therapy had been beneficial."

Therapist I. G., an eclectic psychotherapist who is influenced primarily by Erik Erikson, uses the physics concept of torque as an analogy for the tendency of things to have a motion of their own and to play themselves out. She believes that psychotherapy plays itself out but admits, "Of all the things in the world that are difficult for me, termination is one of the most difficult." When discussing the perfect termination, she says, "Ideally, there would be a sense of accomplishment, having reached a goal. The client would be able to articulate feelings and needs and also feel his or her own inner strength. I don't think termination is a fixed state—it's part of an ongoing cycle like growth. It's not finite; it is a constantly changing and moving continuum."

Therapist J. S., who was trained in psychoanalysis but has become increasingly eclectic, brings up the idea of a follow-up session after a tentative termination. "I feel very strongly that the client should always be the one to initiate termination, so that is how my ideal would begin. The person would come to understand why he or she did things that interfered with feeling good or caused symptoms to develop. The client would have—after understanding the whys—practiced new behavior and been successful at it for a significant period of time. Patients would feel strong and very accepting of their feelings. A process would go on between the patient and the therapist that would celebrate, affirm, and reinforce the changes made and the mutual agreement about terminating treatment. The patient would be out on his or her own for a while, approximately a month, and come back for us to see if it's time to stop completely. I like building in this kind of check and follow-up."

According to therapist D. D., who labeled himself as classical psychoanalytic with a bit of Kohut's psychology of the self, his ideal termination "would be the logical conclusion to a detailed, dynamic treatment. The final stage would be reached at its own pace, no matter how long it took. The therapist would know in an intuitive way. The patient would be an ally, a cotraveler who would be brought into the final plan." He goes on to say that the length of the ending phase should relate to the treatment length. "During the terminal phase, there should be an articulation and recapitulation of what has transpired in treatment. Also, they should discuss what is likely to go on in the future and concentrate as well on the moment-to-moment experience in the present. A firm date should be set early in the termination phase. It should not be inflexible, but held to more or less, unless there is some definite reason to postpone it." This clinician seems much less focused on the interpersonal meaning of the ending and does not include much self-disclosure or mutual sharing of feelings of affection and loss.

Therapist C. E., an analytically trained clinician who now uses Gestalt and family systems, articulates the ideal extratherapeutic and intratherapeutic termination criteria and process that she would like to unfold. "Two people who have come to see each other as human beings develop caring and loving feelings. The client has developed a spontaneity, a sense of vitality, energy, and aliveness. Other criteria for ending would be the client's ability to take risks, trying new behaviors and assuming more responsibility for his or her self. In the therapeutic sessions, the client would be different with me as well—angry, sad, or elated, but most importantly, not concerned with being a 'good patient.' "

These surveyed therapists come from a great variety of theoretical backgrounds. Although there are some language differences, the substance of the psychodynamic and the humanistic schools seems quite similar. Perhaps this supports the hypothesis that no matter what their theoretical approach, as clinicians mature, the treatment they provide becomes less differentiated. Also, there may be significant differences between what many therapists say when queried about their theories and how they practice behind closed doors.

The differences between the ideal and real at times are vast and can cause therapists to strive for overly ambitious treatment outcomes. One striking omission from these ideal conceptualizations, as well as from the actual practices of these therapists, is the lack of discussion or education about termination in the beginning and middle stages of treatment. This gap in the therapeutic process creates many problems when the end is actually confronted or the client slips away, thus continuing the collaborative denial of the ending.

The termination stage is characterized by a mixture of feelings, among them sadness, confusion, and joy. The tasks are numerous and difficult. They include understanding endings as a psychological experience, recapitulating the treatment experience, obtaining closure and letting go, and finally, the ultimate freedom of experiencing new beginnings. No other stage in treatment or in life, for that matter, challenges us more.

2

Who Should Initiate Termination?

The question of who actually initiates the end of the treatment relationship—the therapist or the client—is central to this discussion of termination. According to my formal and informal data as well as my clinical and supervisory experience, the client is usually the first one to bring up the idea of termination. For example, therapist J. W. says: "Termination is almost invariably brought up by my clients. I prefer it that way. If they sound like they are making termination noises, I will reflect this." Therapist R. L. generally leaves the subject up to her clients: "My pattern of termination with somebody is usually played out in the way that they suggest it. The most common example is they begin talking about ending and then my choice is to react to that and make ending a process." Therapist F. B. stated clearly what she considers to be the best situation: "I don't bring up termination. Autonomy is extremely important. The person decided to come and can decide not to come in." My research indicates that most clinicians agree with these sentiments.

Helping clients reach the point where they can chart their own courses is, of course, the ideal treatment goal and leads to ideal terminations. In reality, however, the unique and complex process of psychotherapy is carried out by imper-

26

fect beings with a welter of feelings, attitudes, and values. The labyrinth of emotions stirred up in both practitioner and client during the termination phase makes ending more difficult and important—and ironically, more neglected—than the other psychotherapeutic stages.

Theoretical Opinions Differ

In the literature on terminating therapy, opinions vary widely as to the best way to proceed. Several researchers believe the decision to terminate should be a mutual one between therapist and patient (Gottman and Lieblum, 1974; Lowenberg, 1977; Schiff, 1962). Dewald (1964) writes: "In the ideal situation for insight psychotherapy it [termination] is undertaken at a time considered optimal for the patient's needs and it involves a mutual decision by the patient and therapist" (p. 102).

Among those who believe the initial mention of termination needs to come from the patient is Robbins (1975), who suggests that the patient should make the first move to terminate therapy, but the decision to stop should be a joint agreement. Pumpian-Mindlin (1955) concurs because this sequence of events minimizes the patient's anxiety level. A. Goldberg (1975), a self psychology theorist, clearly demonstrates by his case illustrations that he prefers his clients to initiate termination and he seldom, if ever, interferes with their decisions. It may be that practitioners of Goldberg's theoretical philosophy, like those of the humanistic/phenomenological school, adhere to client-initiated endings in practice as well as in theory more than do followers of other schools of thought.

In contrast, Ferenczi (1955 [1927]) takes the position that analysis will die if the transference neurosis can be resolved. Presumably it is the therapist who decides whether the resolution is complete. Ferenczi also holds that therapy should be terminated when the analyst fails to remain neutral. Reich (1973) reveals that Ferenczi opposed a client's decision to terminate, saying that when a patient wants to leave analysis, he or she is hiding something neurotic. Glover (1955)

also favors a therapist's decision to terminate, calling attention to factors outside the therapeutic alliance, such as the
therapist's caseload.

According to Freud (1963), the therapist should at times
set a fixed date for termination in order to accelerate the treatment process. Referring to one of his own client's reactions
to a predetermined ending date, he wrote: "His resistances
crumbled away, and in the last month of treatment he was
able to produce all the memories and to discover the connecting links which were necessary for the understanding of his
early neurosis and his recovery from the illness from which
he was suffering" (p. 235). Freud's ambivalence about this
technique, however, is apparent in his later reference to it as
a "blackmailing device," although he qualified this comment
by saying that "the measure is effective, provided that one
hits the right time at which to employ it" (p. 235). Firestein
(1978) stated, "One gains the impression that the setting
of the date makes termination more real to the analysand"
(p. 238).

Levinson (1977) maintains that it is most useful for
practitioner and client to mutually set a termination date;
however, there are times when it may be in the client's best
interest to have the practitioner assume responsibility even
when the client does not concur. Applebaum and Holzman
(1967) describe a patient who made tremendous gains in treatment after a self-imposed termination date was established.
"She began to work hard at self-examination in the treatment.
From that time to the end of treatment, a period of almost six
months, every area of her life which had been a problem
improved—she got along more harmoniously with her husband, her children, her parents; she dieted appropriately; physical symptoms diminished; and she experienced increasing
self-esteem, hopefulness, and ambition" (p. 277).

In part, the authors explain this as a divergent form of
the "strangers on a train" phenomenon: "People are for-
tuitously brought together and understand that their relationship is only temporary. Since they have a limited time
together and the relationship is unlikely to have consequences

beyond the trip, they can permit themselves more freedom to become involved with each other and to reveal intimate aspects of their lives than is usual between strangers" (Applebaum and Holzman, 1967, pp. 280–281). Thus, end setting is a technique that can test reality for clients and help them face the inevitability that ending is a real event. It most likely has a similar effect on clinicians.

Perlman (1970) suggests, however, that clients and therapists seldom arrive at a mutually agreed-upon termination date because the clients frequently drop out of treatment, even in the midst of turmoil. The Koss study (1979) of the length of treatment for clients seen in private practice supported this with its finding that a full 80 percent of clients left before receiving twenty-five sessions; the median length of sessions was eight. Garfield (1971), in an extensive review of the duration of treatment in various clinics, concluded that the average number of visits to a psychiatrist is five. From a psychoanalytic viewpoint, such studies provide statistical evidence of the overwhelming trend toward "premature termination" that is partly responsible for the emergence of brief psychotherapy.

Many authors (Klein, 1950; Reich, 1973) favor a gradual weaning of the client from therapy, a process that resembles the behavioral technique called "fading." Bolen (1972) states: "In its ideal mode, termination is structured as a gradual weaning of the client from the relationship with the worker: this weaning is consciously engineered by both of them with attention to the problems encountered" (p. 519).

Jung (1954 [1935]) uses the process of interrupting treatment periodically to encourage his clients' move toward autonomy. Alexander (1963) also discusses a method of "experimental temporary interruptions" aimed at increasing productivity in treatment. Masterman (1976) suggests that "termination be graduated, the therapist being available at later times should the patient require it" (p. 105). Gottman and Lieblum (1974) favor a "phasing out," which gives clients increasing responsibility for monitoring their behavior while encouraging practitioners to program their own behavior and decrease interventions. Buxbaum (1950) argues for an individualized ending based on the characteristics of the client, although no specifications or guidelines are given. Blanck and Blanck (1974) oppose a gradual termination: "We do not advocate tampering with the frequency of sessions. . . . When the patient is ready to terminate he should do so and not prolong dependency by 'tapering' " (p. 388).

Wolberg (1972) notes that the client may want to return to therapy at a later time. Jung felt strongly that therapy should not be restricted by time limits and that termination need not be final. He wrote: "There is no change that is unconditionally valid over a period of time. Life has always to be tackled anew" (1966 [1916], p. 72). Pumpian-Mindlin (1955), Dewald (1964), Hollender (1965), and Rapoport (1970) also support an open-door policy. Ticho (reported in Robbins, 1975), however, cautions against the practitioner providing reassurance that he or she will be available for future consultation, indicating that this conveys the practitioner's doubts about the client's willingness to grow.

Terminations Initiated by Therapists

From the review of the literature and an examination of theoretical perspectives, it appears that therapist-initiated terminations are less common than client-initiated ones. In my own research, also, most therapists indicated that they wait for their clients to bring up termination. However, several practitioners reported that they had introduced the idea of ending. As therapist S. L. states: "I terminate people who are not into seriously working or where I feel I'm not going to be successful. I'm not into hanging on to people. . . . I'm good at this [termination]. I've had wonderful experiences. First of all, I let go of my own children and that's a real growth process."

I hypothesize that many therapist-initiated terminations (ruling out events such as death, moving, or retirement) are related to countertransference issues aroused within the therapist. In this discussion and throughout this work, countertransference is defined as any feeling, issue, or attitude coming from the practitioner that interferes with the treatment process. "Not hanging on" can be a positive attribute, but a therapist's need to "be successful" should not be the criterion for when to terminate.

Even statements such as "the therapy was going nowhere," "we were at an impasse," "the patient was overly dependent," are in my opinion rationalizations to cover up countertransference issues. Certainly, patients have the right to act out all of these psychological issues on the therapeutic stage, even and especially being boring, being stuck, being overly dependent, and all their variants.

It is also fair to acknowledge that it is all right for therapists to have negative feelings about their patients. Whether they should initiate termination because they have not come to grips with their own personal issues, however, is quite another matter. When having trouble handling an overly dependent client, for example, the therapist's task might be to arrange a consultation rather than to rationalize that termination is a proper means of dealing with the problem. If there are no cues or suggestions of termination coming from the patient, and no clearly observable criteria, then a therapist-initiated ending may well be based in countertransference.

There are situations, of course, in which practitioners run into problems they cannot or choose not to work through in their own personal treatment or in consultation. It should be evident within approximately two to twelve sessions whether a clinician is going to be able to work with a particular client. If, after an extended period of time, the therapist feels it is impossible to go on, then a direct and forthright discussion is essential, in which the practitioner must take full responsibility for the situation. The therapist does this by declaring that his or her inability to work with the client does not mean that the client is at fault for lack of progress, but rather that the clinician has some difficulty in the area being addressed in treatment. If the therapist has clearly made the decision without input from the patient, he or she needs to be as self-disclosing as possible about why treatment cannot continue.

The major task here is for the therapist to make an extreme effort to cushion the injury to the patient's self-esteem that such a termination will have. Certainly this should not be a one-session discussion. The clinician needs to fight the impulse to get rid of the patient, as well as deal with his or her own sense of failure and loss of self-esteem. I have observed that such countertransference terminations happen far too often and are destructive to the patient's sense of self. Explanation and consultation are essential to a countertransference termination being handled well.

Deleterious Therapist-Initiated Terminations. Three examples of unsuccessful therapist-initiated countertransference terminations follow. These case studies are true, and events like these are more common than practitioners might like to admit. Given that it is easy to criticize after the fact, such examples may yet be useful for learning purposes, particularly since there is very little explicit, practical literature on the subject of termination. (Few clinicians write about their treatment failures, especially in the termination phase.)

Margaret R., a thirty-eight-year-old executive, was seen twice a week in psychodynamic psychotherapy by Dr. Janet P., a well-seasoned clinician. Treatment with this severely characterologically disturbed individual had gone on for a year and a half, and although Dr. P. reported that she frequently had feelings of dislike for this patient, she believed they could continue to work together. "But I started to feel increasingly angry with her. She was intruding on my life, actually calling frequently and even following me once. That was the final straw. I told her that I could not work with her anymore." Ms. R. felt victimized, helpless, and rageful. They met twice more and then Dr. P. referred her to a colleague.

What can be learned from this therapist-initiated countertransference termination? First, even well-educated, impeccably trained, intelligent practitioners make mistakes. In a review of the case, the following data emerged: Those nagging feelings of not liking the patient should have been attended to because they were the key to Dr. P.'s increasingly negative countertransference feelings. Physically and emotionally, this patient reminded the clinician of her own mother, who had been an extremely angry, controlling, intrusive, non-nurturing person. This remained just out of Dr. P.'s awareness most of the time she was treating Ms. R., possibly to protect her own self.

If she had not felt guilty about her personal reaction toward the patient, one of two positive actions could have been taken: Dr. P. might have decided she could not work with this individual and made an appropriate referral early in treatment, or she could have accepted the case and then made a strong commitment to explore, work through, and grow personally from the experience in very close supervision. Either path would have been acceptable. Certainly the intense emotional pain that resulted could have been avoided for both patient and practitioner.

I believe that the interactive process of transference/countertransference escalated until Dr. P. was too overwhelmed to provide a good treatment experience. Both patient and practitioner were enmeshed in a series of mutually unhealthy interactions. Ending treatment became Dr. P.'s way of avoiding personal exploration and took on importance as an issue of psychological survival for her.

In a second example of therapist-initiated countertransference termination, we see a similar pattern unfold. Jack F., a twenty-eight-year-old professional man, was in treatment for ten months with Dr. Barry W., a competent therapist. The presenting problems were anxiety, depression, and very low self-esteem. According to Dr. W., this was a difficult case from the onset. Mr. F. would frequently experience suicidal feelings and intense emotional responses centering around rejection and abandonment. Diagnostically, he would be considered a borderline personality who was able to function at a reasonable level at work and in superficial social situations, although he had never formed a lasting relationship.

When I interviewed Dr. W., he was able to articulate some of his fears, anxieties, and frustrations related to several strong countertransference issues. "I had given up hope. I began to believe him, that there was no hope—a part of me felt the best thing for him to do was to die." Dr. W. said that his countertransference reaction seemed based on his own early experiences with his mother, whom he perceived as characterologically similar to the patient—clinging, demanding, easily hurt, asking to be taken care of but rejecting help. "I felt I had two choices—to stop seeing him or get back into my own personal treatment."

Dr. W. chose to end the therapeutic relationship, but I feel he made the wrong choice for the patient as well as himself. When he found that personal issues were interfering with his ability to function therapeutically, it might have been better if he had obtained a supervisory consultation. Consider how devastated this patient felt after experiencing yet another rejection: His worst fears had become real. When told that Dr. W. was ending therapy with him, Mr. F. said, "I can understand why you want to get rid of me."

There are several important similarities in these two cases. Both practitioners unknowingly acted out a recapitulation of their patients' early experiences with caretakers because of their own unresolved personal issues. Dr. P. and Dr. W. experienced these patients' issues as narcissistic injuries. Each patient exhibited an intense affect (anger, frustration, self-destruction). Most therapists do have a particular affect with which they have trouble dealing and which they experience as an injury to their self-structure. To maintain their own self-esteem, I believe that both Dr. P. and Dr. W. worked—at an unconscious level—to rid themselves of the source of the injuries—the patients.

These situations are examples of a clinician's inability to truly empathize with a patient's disturbing and painful emotions. Kohut (1984) writes that most treatment failures are due to these human limitations. Although no one can achieve perfect empathy, the goal should always be to approximate it as closely as possible.

The following case illustrates a variation of the therapist-initiated termination that is difficult to categorize, although it is obvious that the therapist is acting out many countertransference issues.

Lisa C., a very anxious twenty-nine-year-old woman, had been in psychodynamic and open-ended treatment for approximately thirteen months with Dr. Stephanie V., a well-trained psychotherapist. The patient felt that her therapy was not going well and finally was able to timidly express her doubts to the therapist. Dr. V. responded angrily and defensively, saying if Ms. C. wasn't happy with treatment, she could end it immediately. The therapist seemed to experience an injury to her own self-esteem that prevented her from trying to understand what her patient was feeling. As usual, this iatrogenic termination began with a nonempathic posture on the part of the therapist. If Dr. V. had been better in touch with her client and had a stronger grasp of her own countertransference issues, she would have understood what Ms. C. was feeling and used this in a helpful way. Instead, Ms. C. became a psychotherapy casualty by having a professional therapist reinforce her worst fears and feelings.

Positive Therapist-Initiated Terminations. Is it ever appropriate for the practitioner to be the one to end the therapeutic relationship? Yes, although therapist-initiated terminations not based on countertransference are rare. When the therapist, who has been empathically listening, picks up on unverbalized termination cues (see Chapter Three for a discussion of this criterion), he or she can initiate the issue of ending by reflecting these feelings to the patient. For example, the therapist might say, "I've been feeling that ending therapy has been on your mind for a while."

In the case that follows, maximum treatment gains were achieved successfully although the client had not verbally initiated termination. Roy D., a forty-four-year-old marketing consultant, had been in treatment for almost three years with Dr. Herb G., a respected psychotherapist. The client, who had entered treatment with moderate depression and low self-esteem, stated that his goal was to have closer relationships with others, especially a long-term relationship with a woman. His reasons for seeking psychotherapy and his personal goals were compatible with the therapist's diagnosis of narcissistic personality disorder and treatment goals for him. This is an essential precondition for a productive treatment and, specifically, a healthy termination. If therapist and client cannot agree overtly on treatment goals, how will they ever decide on how and when to end therapy?

For the first eighteen months, Mr. D. attended sessions on a twice-weekly schedule. Treatment helped him a great deal. The therapist related: "So many areas of his life were going so well for a continued period. He really had done what he came to do. He started coming in once a week and continued to do well. I was increasingly feeling from him that he was getting ready to terminate. So I reflected this— that I was wondering if he had been thinking about ending. The client said he had been thinking about it for quite a while but felt awkward about getting it out." Dr. G. and Mr. D. continued to talk about and work toward termination for several more months until their relationship came to a natural and mutually satisfying closure.

This was a healthy, evolutionary, appropriate therapist-initiated termination because of many factors. Most essential is that there was a mutually agreed-upon agenda for treatment from the first session and throughout all phases of therapy. In addition, the therapist initiated termination in response to the client's feeling, which he perceived, through "projective introspection," or empathy. Dr. G. was not acting out a countertransference issue to fulfill a need of his own, other than the need to be an ethical psychotherapist. In fact, he had enjoyed working with Mr. D., who was interesting and likable, particularly as he grew healthier, who hardly ever had a crisis, and who paid him on time. Since letting go of valued clients is often more painful than giving up difficult patients, it was a measure of the therapist's own emotional health that he was able to terminate this model client in such a positive fashion.

If the therapist does not process this issue like all others but, instead, elects to wait for the patient to verbalize, he or she runs the risk of being perceived by this patient as hanging on too long or of giving the subtle message that the client is not growing. Although timing is a very important part of the treatment process, even if it is not perfect—and it seldom is—a forthright discussion can be extremely helpful, especially if it is conducted with sound therapeutic technique, principles, and skills, just as the preceding months of therapy have been.

Terminations Initiated by Clients

As discussed above, in spite of the variety of opinions from every psychotherapeutic school of thought, most terminations are initiated by the clients. There are two main types of these endings: the positive one in which the client initiates termination and the therapist agrees, and the deleterious one in which the client brings it up and the therapist does not agree.

Positive Client-Initiated Terminations. A termination that the client initiates and the practitioner supports is, in my opinion, the most optimal model for the ending of a therapeutic relationship. In such a situation the patient has felt healed and healthier for a relatively continuous period of time. This can translate into various operational definitions or criteria, which will be discussed later. The patient brings up the idea of ending the sessions and the therapist, who also believes it is an appropriate time to begin the termination process, agrees. As therapist A. K. responds, "I don't think I would ever disagree with a client who wanted to discontinue treatment. You must assume that if someone brings it [termination] up, they have reasons. I'm comfortable if I understand their reasons. If I don't understand them, I respect them anyway."

Actually, "beginning the termination process" is something of a misnomer since the process of ending treatment, if it is carried out in the correct spirit and philosophy, should start at the moment of inception. Therapist M. J. says it best: "As a rule, I try to discuss termination throughout treatment. It's tied in with a kind of educational process—discussing with clients that there are different layers of treatment and people stop at different points and decide when and if they should return to treatment," Not only is this a wonderful philosophy whose practical implementation is much too rare, but it is especially good because it espouses a no-blame situation that allows and encourages the client's autonomy and self-direction. It is compatible with Jung's (1954 [1935]) perspective of not fostering unnecessary dependency.

The psychotherapeutic relationship, unique and intricate as it is, is also defined as time-limited: It begins when two people come together to ultimately separate. The task of the therapist, depending on his or her theoretical orientation and the client's goals and needs, can range from maintenance with a psychotic patient to helping a healthy, functioning person become more self-actualized and proactive. The job of the patient is only to participate in as honest a way possible to achieve these objectives.

The practitioner, being the paid professional, must strive toward maintaining a therapeutic posture that not only helps the patient grow and change but also does not infantilize or create unnecessary dependencies. Thus, from the onset of treatment, the relationship begins to end. When a practitioner does not understand this concept, or enters a therapeutic relationship without keeping it in mind, serious problems can arise. My research suggests that, tragically, this happens too often.

Another reason "beginning the termination process" is a misnomer is that before the conscious awareness and subsequent verbalization about the ending of treatment occurs, an unconscious process has been unfolding at another level for some time.

My optimal model of termination is partly grounded in the humanistic school of thought exemplified by Carl Rogers and the client-centered therapy approach. This philosophy is based on the idea that clients are unique, proactive beings striving toward growth, change, and self-actualization. In most interactions within the therapeutic context, including termination, patients need to be viewed as capable of choosing their own destinies and treated with dignity and respect. Thus, this optimal termination model assumes—even though it is essential to individualize each case—that psychotherapy patients should be treated as autonomous adults, not sick children. This is true even when patients behave in infantile or less-than-healthy ways.

Two cases illustrate how the humanistic philosophy shapes the way practitioners can respond respectfully to their patients' desires to terminate. Gene L., a thirty-six-year-old construction worker entered therapy because of depressed feelings and a general feeling of being "discontented" with his life. He had been married and divorced three times, an indication of his trouble with commitment and intimacy. He wanted to be less depressed and to just feel better. His experienced therapist, Joanne Y., conceptualized his depression as the result of lowered self-esteem resulting from the loss of yet another relationship.

Mr. L., as one would expect, acted out his fear of intimacy, dependency, and commitment with Ms. Y., but she was able to weather his emotional storms and help him heal. His terror of being dependent and subsequently engulfed or abandoned caused him to bring up termination on numerous occasions. Ms. Y. would reflect his fears and try to maintain an empathic posture—not verbally agreeing or disagreeing. As Mr. L.'s sense of self became more cohesive, his depression slowly lifted. After one and three-quarters years of therapy, he brought up termination in a qualitatively different manner, stating that he no longer was depressed and generally felt good about himself and was thinking about ending therapy. Ms. Y. agreed, affirming his progress and growth. Two months later they parted.

It should be emphasized that even when the therapist did not really believe that termination was appropriate, she did not disagree with him. I am convinced that her empathic attitude—nonjudgmental, noncritical, and nondirective—enabled the patient to continue the healing process. This set the tone for a positive treatment experience and, eventually, a successful termination when the therapist agreed and actually felt that the time for ending was appropriate. Thus her feelings and ideas about the case matched what she verbalized to the patient.

In the second example, the client initiates termination and his therapist agrees verbally but does not concur intuitively or cognitively. Richard K., a forty-five-year-old father of three children, sought treatment because of anxiety attacks that were becoming increasingly severe. Within six months he was showing marked improvement, so he started to bring up termination. Dr. James H. believed, however, that there was still more work to do. "I felt the underlying causes of anxiety were not fully dealt with, although the patient had accomplished what he set out to do."

Thus, the therapist did not let his goals interfere with the patient's initial expressed treatment goal or his movement toward individuation and self-cohesion. Although Dr. H. did not wholeheartedly encourage his client to terminate, he also did not interfere or try to manipulate him, either directly or subtly. Subsequently, Mr. K. terminated with very good feelings about himself, the therapist, and the treatment experience. He also knew he could return at any time if he needed to.

Deleterious Client-Initiated Terminations. When the client initiates the termination and the therapist verbally disagrees, the result is the most complex and potentially painful and negative type of ending. These occur when countertransference issues are stirred up within the practitioner; indeed, my data showed a number of familiar patterns, including the dependent therapist, the defensive one, the hurt one, and the controlling one, all of which are discussed in this work.

Before examining some of these variations, let us explore the general question of whether a therapist *should* disagree with a patient's decision to terminate. My research suggests that practitioners generally believe that it is better for the treatment ending if therapists do not initiate termination, and I concur in this opinion. Further, in most cases, they should not verbally disagree with a client's decision to terminate, even if they do not believe it is appropriate to end treatment. There is much to lose and little to gain from the practitioner interjecting personal feelings and needs into the termination decision. Usually, confrontation serves no valuable purpose in psychotherapy and, specifically, is usually a detriment to the termination process. Conversely, respect for the patient's autonomy and self-growth is crucial.

One of the best reasons for agreeing with the client is that disagreeing is not therapeutic or helpful. If the patient brings up thoughts and feelings about ending therapy and the therapist disagrees for any reason, the therapeutic relationship—assuming it was a good one—is frequently irrevocably damaged or flawed. This is true even if the practitioner disagrees in a seemingly nonintrusive and well-intended manner.

My own traditional training included very little on the subject of termination. However, I was taught to disagree by interpretation if I thought a patient was not ready to terminate. In reality, however, as well as through my research, I have found that although disagreement sometimes persuades clients to stay longer, more often it actually sabotages the treatment process. Such an issue touches the core, the sense of oneself as a self-directed human being. This is especially true for psychotherapy clients seen in outpatient, private practice settings who are being treated in open-ended, psychodynamic psychotherapy, and who, in the majority of cases, are suffering from various disorders of the self. Even if clients manipulate therapists into making decisions for them, therapists must try to maintain respect for their patients' autonomy and avoid being demigods or indulging in manipulative interpretation.

Unfortunately, such matches between clients who struggle with growing up emotionally and therapists who gain a great deal from directing their patients' lives are too common an occurrence, as the following cases illustrate.

Barbara P., a twenty-seven-year-old incest victim, reported after many months of twice-a-week sessions that she tentatively said to her psychotherapist, Dr. Dennis E., "I have been considering ending therapy for quite some time now." Dr. E.'s response was, "We can talk about that later." He then initiated a discussion about her father's recent visit. Dr. E. was refusing to deal with termination at all. Instead, he chose to bring up the client's most emotionally charged issue, which distracted both of them from the task at hand—to explore the client's feelings about termination. When asked in a research interview about her reaction to his response, Ms. P. answered, "This was not the first time that this had happened. Each time I introduced the subject, he always brought up my father or some other related problem. I felt exploited, like I did with my father, and I don't think it was in my head. I felt, and I was correct, that he would not discuss it! The only way I was able to end therapy was that my job changed and I started traveling about 80 percent of the time, so he could not accommodate my schedule. I was tremendously relieved because I had felt trapped. Finally I could stop therapy!"

In another case, Mark B., a divorced twenty-five-year-old professional man, entered treatment with Dr. Edith M., an experienced clinician. Mr. B. wanted to explore issues around his marriage and subsequent divorce. He was moderately uncomfortable but certainly not in any crisis or in tremendous psychic pain. He was looking for an insight-oriented psychodynamic treatment experience.

From the onset it was a very good and helpful experience. After about two years, however, Mr. B. felt he had accomplished his goals and began to make termination noises during his sessions with Dr. M. He reported later that working toward ending therapy had been on his mind for a number of months, but he was apprehensive about bringing it up. He remembered making remarks such as "I am starting to feel as though I am not in therapy anymore. I enjoy our sessions, but it feels different." However, these and other comments were ignored by Dr. M.; defensively or selectively, she did not hear his termination noises. One day he finally confronted her directly about the possibility of terminating by saying, "I have been thinking about stopping therapy and I thought maybe we could talk about it."

"Well, there is a great deal of work yet to be done," Dr. J. responded abruptly.

"But," he persisted, "I've been feeling so good and so many things are going well for me."

"Yes, but if you don't deal with some other issues, things could get bad for you later," the therapist argued.

While sessions continued for a month or two, the client never felt the same comfort about treatment and slowly withdrew from the therapeutic relationship.

This case shows clearly that Dr. M. had serious difficulties letting go; she was straying from basic therapeutic principles and techniques. The case also demonstrates the tenacious will clients have to act as independent people. Even through the hurt, anger, and pain, this client was able to experience the positive and freeing aspects of termination as well as an unparalleled sense of surviving the end of a valued relationship and experience.

Another example shows the therapist acting out in a different manner. Ken H., a thirty-three-year-old accountant, had been in open-ended, once-a-week psychotherapy with Franklin S., a prominent psychotherapist, for slightly over two years. One day Mr. H. broached the subject of termination: "I thought we could take some time and talk about it, but I'm pretty sure I want to work toward ending."

Mr. S. responded, "Well, my experience is that talking about it for a time does not help. If you really want to stop, we may as well end today."

The patient was shocked into silence. Only later did he realize the impact of this sudden termination and the hurt, anger, and rejection that he felt. Although he was upset by this ending process, or the lack thereof, he recalled a strong sense of feeling that termination was still the right thing for him at that time. In some ways, the fact that this client could handle so well such a potentially devastating situation showed clearly that he was ready to terminate. The tragedy, however, was that he was robbed of an opportunity to work through his feelings, explore what the termination meant to him, and accelerate his development by discussing areas that needed more work or review. A crucial factor for this patient is that he had a fairly intact self structure before the onset of treatment, which was made more cohesive by the therapeutic experience. What if he had been more disturbed, had had a severe personality disorder, or had been a borderline personality, which is frequently the case in long-term, open-ended psychotherapy? Obviously, the result would have been more devastating. Doubtless it is the very fragile patient who is most vulnerable to the therapeutic unconscious or conscious exploitation of termination issues.

Examples of client-initiates–therapist-disagrees terminations are unfortunately fairly common. Many other cases in this book illustrate the deleterious results that can follow when a practitioner disagrees with a patient's decision to move toward ending treatment. Theodore Reich (1973) spoke of therapists needing to listen with the "third ear," thus using all their senses, including intuition, to help grasp the essence of their patients' communications. It could be said that too often when the issue of ending treatment is at hand, therapists listen with only one ear.

The traditionally trained practitioner might say that the expression of the wish to terminate is a resistance to deeply repressed material and that the therapist is right to confront this. This reasoning, however, leaves the client in a no-win situation: His or her feelings are not respected but are used as indications against the feasibility of termination. This typifies a certain therapist-as-demigod attitude ("I know better about yourself than you") and displays a nonempathic understanding of the patient. If the practitioner respects the client's autonomy, a positive termination and thus a successful treatment has a chance of evolving.

The key concept is expressed by a client of Sue Chance, M.D., (1987) in this comment on ending treatment: "You know why we worked so well together, Dr. Chance?" her client says. "It was because I respected you and you respected me" (p. 21). Although simply stated, the words connote a powerful message: Therapists are more apt to receive respect if they can offer it in a deep and felt manner. Sometimes, however, they may provide it for years to patients and still not get it back—this is an occupational hazard practitioners must learn to work through. The more cohesively formed their own sense of self is, the better equipped they are to tolerate disrespectful endings.

Separation, loss, and abandonment are all crucial to the continuing quest for a fully developed self structure. Chance's client wrote: "Nothing lasts forever, but I did have the grace of having you step in my life for a short time when everything seemed impossible. . . . You should be proud of your accomplishments with me. Saying goodbye is hard, but since you've left a part of you with me, I'll never forget you. Thank you for taking me by the hand for a brief period, until I could walk on my own" (p. 21).

3

Exploring Key Criteria
for Ending Therapy

The termination process, analogous to the whole course of a client's psychotherapy, has both overt and covert aspects that cannot be understood simply by observing the final sessions. The patient and the practitioner participate in a series of verbal and nonverbal interactions over time that communicate whether the client feels ready for termination and whether the therapist feels the client is at a point where termination is indicated. Before any verbalization about the ending of treatment occurs, each partner engages the other in a complex series of cues, signs, and interactions that assess each other's reactions to the emerging feelings. Most experienced practitioners have a list of such cues or criteria, both conscious and unconscious, that they watch for and use to gauge readiness to end the therapeutic relationship.

Types of Criteria

Therapists' major criteria for the ending of treatment, as seen in the literature and my own research, include intuition, symptom relief, improved intrapsychic and interpersonal functioning, resolution of transference, and dreams.

Intuition. Practitioner intuition is an important guideline for terminating therapy. Intuitive criteria, although difficult if not impossible to objectify, play an important part in many psychodynamic psychotherapists' decisions about ending treatment.

Glover (1955) and other researchers (Firestein, 1978; Levenson, 1976; Schiff, 1962) agree that intuition is a key factor in judgments concerning termination. Glover defines intuition as "a feeling or impression that the end was approaching" (p. 327); in his study of psychoanalysts' attitudes toward termination, the majority of therapists he surveyed use intuition as their criterion for termination. Held (in Firestein, 1978) discusses termination in terms of telepathic communication. Krebs (1972) develops a criterion related to intuition that he terms "focusing": "When the client says he is doing better . . . I immediately start focusing inside myself. 'How does that feel to me? Is it really okay if he stops?' " (p. 360).

In my first study, therapist D. D. stated that "the therapist would know in an intuitive way" when it is time to end treatment, and "the patient would be an ally, a cotraveler who would be brought into the final plan."

Symptom Relief. "Patients would either be free of the symptoms that initially had them start therapy or feel they were greatly reduced or much more manageable," says therapist J. S. Relief from symptoms or significant change in symptomatology, since it relates directly to what brings clients to treatment, should have more credence in the eyes of practitioners than it generally does. Owing to the influence of classical analytic theory and folklore, it has been reduced to a second-class criterion, connoting an inferior or inadequate treatment.

As Nunberg (1954) states, "patients appreciate symptom relief more than character change" (p. 3), and many authors (Epstein, 1980; Glover, 1955; Schiff, 1962; Siporin, 1975; Weigert, 1952) agree that this can be a clear sign of approaching termination. Wolberg (1972) cautions, however, that although patients may regard symptomatic relief as the best measure of positive gain, it is not a reliable index of therapeutic success.

Improved Intrapsychic Functioning. Variations on common themes of improvement in client functioning, both intrapsychic and interpersonal, form the basis of a group of criteria used by the ego psychology theorists and the structuralists.

Ego psychologists look for improved autonomous ego functioning; improved interpersonal, social, or object relations (increased ability to love); and an increased sense of self or identity. Termination should thus take place when a client's ego is sufficiently developed to withstand unhappiness and maintain resiliency. Hartmann (1964) states that "a healthy person must be able to suffer and be depressed" (p. 6). Freud (1957) discusses therapeutic progress in terms of "whether the subject is left with a sufficient capacity for enjoyment and efficiency" (vol. 16, p. 457). Thus, the patient's abilities to love and work are important outcome criteria for many psychodynamic practitioners. Attainment of identity, a strong and better functioning ego, object constancy, neutralization of the drives, and other developmental accomplishments form Blanck and Blanck's (1974) basis for termination criteria. Klein's (1950) rationale requires that persecutory and depressive anxiety should be sufficiently reduced to produce a capacity for love.

The structuralists adhere to a classical Freudian model of reorganizing the client's id, ego, and superego (Freud, 1923). They focus on the patient's ability to tolerate stress and experience pleasure. In opposition to the ego psychology school, they analyze the instinctual drives and wishes based in the id that are deeply repressed and unconscious. They emphasize the importance of the process of treatment and the desirable effects of positive treatment. The structural and ego-psychology-based criteria share many of the same difficulties in terms of reliability as the symptomatic criteria. In addition, they rely even more on the clinician's subjective interpretation and less on the patient's own valuation. As therapist A. T. simply states, one of his criteria for termination is "people feeling better about their 'selves' " so that they exhibit freedom of behavior and feelings.

Resolution of Transference. Every psychodynamic approach

to psychotherapy uses as a significant evaluative criterion for the conclusion of treatment the resolving or "working through" of the transference. Although the language is different, humanistic approaches also rely heavily on the patient's ability to see the therapist as a real person. Therapist P. F. looks for changes in the therapeutic relationship as a gauge of change and growth. "Clients would fully acknowledge their relationship with me, expressing their feelings about me, especially what I meant to them. They would see me as a person who remains interested in them beyond my professional role."

Ferenczi (1955 [1927]) typifies authors (Levenson, 1976; Reich, 1973; Ticho, in Robbins, 1975; Weigert, 1952) who feel transference issues are strong indications of ending treatment. Ferenczi believes that by the time of termination, the client should be able to see the therapist as a real person, relate in a less subordinate manner, and be as free as possible from idealizing or deprecating the therapist. He also discusses countertransference as an issue related to termination, saying that therapists must constantly examine their own personality problems to minimize their deleterious influences on the treatment process, particularly those factors that might prolong it.

Dreams. Dreams are sometimes used as signals that termination is approaching. Authors such as Cavenar and Nash (1976) feel this sort of cue is often neglected. Glover (1955) states that "some analysts quite frankly give preference to dream analysis. Either explicitly or implicitly they encourage the patient to begin each session by communicating dreams of the night before" (p. 165). Keiser (in Robbins, 1975) comments that he welcomes the appearance of dreams of rebirth during termination as a reliable barometer of the validity of the final interruption. Saul (1972) also refers to dreams: "Effective progress in dealing with the major emotional forces in the transference and in life such as increased frankness of material and dreams of resolution will make the analyst think of a trial ending" (p. 401).

Dreams alone would be a very unlikely single indicator

for most practitioners, especially those who see patients on a once-or twice-weekly schedule. If dreams are not used as an integral part of the treatment process, it is not expected that they would be regarded as important termination cues.

Therapists' Termination Criteria

While conducting my research and making observations in my own practice, I was repeatedly struck by the discrepancies between theoretical discussions of termination criteria and their practical application—or nonapplication—in clinical situations. Exploring the issue from the practitioners' point of view (patients do not have a gap between theory and practice), what factors do therapists regard as criteria for ending therapy?

Practitioners' responses to specific questions about their termination practices range from the general (felt better) and abstract (worked through unconscious issues) to the specific (trusted spouse more). In more than half the responses, the therapists referred to some type of global improvement factor such as "handling life well," "doing much better," or "greatly improved in all areas." Also important to therapists in approximately the same proportions were the two categories specific intrapsychic or internal improvement factors (improved self-esteem or a resolution of the patient's Oedipal conflict) and specific external or observable improvement factors (the patient's ability to form a lasting intimate relationship or obtain career success). As therapist U. C. states, "The patient is pleased with what has happened, has worked out basic conflicts, and can live a more gratifying life."

There appears to be nothing unexpected about the responses. Of interest, however, is another category that emerged, the cost/benefit ratio, which is also consonant with the clients' termination criteria. Various therapists discuss it in different ways. The essence is that gradually it becomes apparent that the emotional time and monetary cost factors are not in balance with the relative benefit a client receives. Therapist M. J. explains: "When the time and money spent seeing me would probably produce no further worthwhile gain, then it is time to terminate."

When clinicians encourage their clients to evaluate whether they are getting enough out of the relationship, they may foster self-development and contribute to clients' independence. For example, Andrea L., a twenty-five-year-old word processor, began therapy with Mr. Michael H., showing multiple symptoms and difficulties. Her formal diagnosis was borderline personality disorder. She was extremely regressed at the onset of treatment and close to being hospitalized. Almost immediately she became intensely dependent on the therapist while being afraid of her dependent feelings. In both the beginning and middle stages of treatment, Ms. L. could not imagine ever living without Mr. H. or their sessions. He attempted to empathically reflect her feelings and eventually planted the seeds of her surviving and actually feeling proud of her emerging independent feelings. In the evolutionary manner described above, Ms. L. began to wonder, first in fantasy and later in reality, about life after therapy. She eventually was able to weigh the benefits against the cost of therapy. Her newly formed, more cohesive self structure enabled her to examine what she was getting from her therapy, both positively and negatively. If her therapist had suffered from termination countertransference issues and not supported her independence, she might have been a lifelong and interminable patient.

Another interesting finding was the small frequency with which therapists gave responses to the broader category of decrease in presenting problems. The paucity of statements on this important set of termination criteria is perhaps a symptom of the therapists' confusion about termination and the underlying countertransference issues. Psychodynamic therapists, in general, seem to be more comfortable with abstract phenomena such as intrapsychic change than with symptom alleviation and the reduction of presenting problems or complaints. Psychodynamic philosophy teaches therapists that they know the patients' "needs" better than the patients know themselves. Usually this translates into more therapy than the patient thinks is necessary. Therapists need to consider that more is not necessarily better and that decreasing or alleviating symptoms is not insignificant.

Thus, if a patient says, "I am thinking about stopping therapy because my anxiety attacks seem to be under control," this is both important and desirable. The practitioner's responsibility is not merely to support such growth but to actively be on the lookout for it. Self-actualized and well-informed practitioners should be thinking, "This patient is doing great. She has not had an anxiety attack in a long time. Perhaps we should be thinking about termination." Moreover, rather than plant seeds of doubt or insecurity, the practitioner needs to reflect this growth and change to the patient, thus adding to her emerging and more cohesive self.

The difficulties that originally bring a patient into the clinician's office are frequently forgotten as the treatment goes on. In the course of a protracted, open-ended treatment, it is easy to be caught up in the process and lose sight of the presenting problems. Therapists who remember why the patient sought psychotherapy and who affirm even moderate growth, especially as it relates to the original problem, keep important guideposts in sight for themselves as well as for their clients. This growth or change is a significant general criterion for ending therapy and is the essence of the spirit and philosophy that should guide practitioners who conduct open-ended psychotherapy.

Clients' Termination Criteria

When clients initiate termination, many of their criteria are similar to those of their therapists. The following categories emerged from my study: treatment unsatisfactory, cost/benefit ratio, external factors, global improvement factors, specific external or observable improvement factors, specific intrapsychic or internal improvement factors, and financial cost.

According to these clients, most termination criteria were substantially related to the category global improvement factors, which includes a group of general references to "feeling better." Approximately half the respondents referred to "specific external or internal factors," citing them independently or in conjunction with a global improvement factor—for example, the decrease of a specific problematic behavior (specific) or increased self-esteem (global). The largest other single criterion these clients say they use in making termination decisions was some form of cost/benefit analysis: further benefit from treatment would not be enough to offset the expenditure of emotional energy and/or financial cost required.

A very small number of clients cited some specific or general dissatisfaction with either the direction therapy was taking or the therapist's behavior. Since most of these analyzed cases were of long-term treatments, it is not surprising that this number is so small. People who stay in treatment for an extended period generally are comfortable with the therapist and most likely tolerant of the therapist's idiosyncrasies.

The criterion of financial cost alone, as opposed to the cost/benefit ratio, was also used with very low frequency. Some classical psychoanalytically oriented practitioners could easily argue that these individuals placed themselves unconsciously in a situation where they would have to end treatment and this probably was a form of resistance. Certainly this happens. Another view is that the client saw no other way of ending therapy. Whether this is true, or whether the patient simply ran out of funds, the financial cost criterion provides a way out for the patient regardless of motivations or feelings, as will be seen in the case of Michael A. in Chapter Five.

When there is a disparity between the therapist's criteria and the client's, the ending may become chaotic. Such a gap in the therapeutic process can create many problems when termination is actually confronted or when the client slips away and a collaborative denial of the inevitable separation continues.

Do Therapists Actually Use Their Criteria?

If clients are not informed in the beginning of the treatment that they should be ready to end therapy when they resolve their Oedipal or instinctual conflicts (conflict theory), develop a cohesive self (defect theory), or become self-actualized (humanistic theory), how can they be expected to conclude therapy properly? Theoretical termination criteria are not useful if only clinicians know about them. This problem is further compounded when the therapist does not agree that it is time to stop and then—at that late date—explains the guidelines for leaving therapy.

It is important enough to repeat the idea that patient-identified issues should be the focus of therapy, not therapists' preconceived theories. As therapist C. R. reported, "From the outset of therapy, the patients should identify what the major problems and issues are, how they would like to be different, and what they need to do to change." Whether a patient's stated problems can be labeled an Oedipal issue or a faulty self structure, the practitioner's task is to help this person obtain his or her goals and to avoid focusing excessively on theoretical criteria—the practitioner's agenda. A therapist who lets the primacy of theory replace an individualized treatment approach makes a serious error from which many treatments never recover: That treatment becomes the therapist's and not the client's.

For example, if a patient comes to treatment with a specific desire to work on an eating disorder such as bulimia, there is no conflict if the therapist conceptualizes the problem as a faulty self structure that needs to be made more cohesive and firm. The therapist is using theory and experience to derive a treatment plan. In this example, the therapist's termination criteria would most likely be an intrapsychic one, the development of a healthy, cohesive, nuclear self. After two years of therapy, the client is symptom-free and brings up the idea of termination. She has done what she set out to do. However, the practitioner believes more therapy is needed because the patient's self structure is not yet developed enough. At this juncture predetermined, perfectionistic, therapist-based termination criteria become part of the problem rather than the solution.

Objective, well-defined, realistic termination criteria

need to be agreed upon by client and therapist at the start of treatment. This must be done, of course, on an individualized basis. Such an approach makes the process of termination a more conscious, overt interchange between client and practitioner instead of the usual covert learning process. With the covert method, the client must somehow learn what the appropriate termination criteria are and then evaluate whether he or she has met them. When the patient says, "I am feeling better. Maybe it's time to talk about ending," the therapist should not respond with his or her first statement about termination criteria. If everything is acted out at an unaware level, termination will remain a process fraught with countertransference issues and confusion, and more treatments will end in an unsatisfying fashion for both patients and practitioners. If the entire process of treatment endings is not made more clear, overt, and practically applicable, then the type of criteria to which a therapist adheres becomes a moot point.

Therapists who practice classical psychoanalysis and psychoanalytically based psychotherapy, more than those who use other approaches, may foster the attitude that "the doctor knows best what the patient needs." Some therapists of this school appear to feel, in general, that patients should not be educated about the therapy process. These practitioners are more at risk for termination problems. "What I look for," stated therapist O. G., "is total characterological change or reorganization. Anything short of this is really not doing the job properly." It was obvious from the subsequent interview that this therapist's crucial expectations were never conveyed to her patients, particularly not at the beginning of treatment. Perhaps if they had been, patients would have chosen another therapist or at least asked for some clarification of "total characterological change." Then there would have been the opportunity for discussion of some reasonably obtainable goals and criteria for ending treatment, in particular, criteria that were important to the client.

In contrast to the traditional analytic view is therapist T. N., a client-centered clinician. He told me that termination should not be treated any differently than other issues in the treatment process: "One needs to listen to the client." He follows the client's lead, allowing and encouraging the client's needs to remain salient factors. For example, one of his patients, after approximately thirty sessions, began the next hour by saying, "I was thinking that I might not need to come in much longer." Therapist T. N. recalls thinking, "I see her as a person who could benefit from coming in for a long time." However, he felt it was more important to respect her feelings and needs. "I believe very strongly in respecting the level that people seek out," he told me. This therapist melds theory and practice: He is literally practicing what he preaches.

Although these two therapeutic approaches can be contrasted in almost every way, neither the analytic nor the client-centered clinician discussed the ending of therapy with their clients at the beginning of the treatment process. This is, however, less of a problem when the therapist does not interfere with a patient's decision to end. The clinician who argues with a client and tries to manipulate the person into staying in treatment because he or she does not agree with the client's termination criteria, will probably lose this patient forever—even if this person stays for a while—because the therapist has violated the patient's right to self-direction. In contrast, the clinician who respects the patient as a proactive human being capable of making choices supports growth and the development of a healthier self. Moreover, the person will probably feel free to come back at another time, if need be.

Many types of rationalization are used by therapists who manipulate their clients into remaining in treatment. At a recent national conference, a prominent psychoanalytic therapist and his disciples boasted of how they relentlessly "confronted" patients when they wanted to "prematurely" end their treatments. This clinician spoke with rigor and sincerity about how it is the job of the therapist to confront the "resistances" of the patient and to interpret the desire to end therapy as "acting out." This sort of unexamined adherence to dogma leads me to wonder who is acting out.

One therapist at the convention described repeatedly phoning a patient, who was severely disturbed (a borderline personality disorder), and insisting in a forceful tone that the patient continue her treatment. The therapist boasted about the efficacy of this confrontational approach and announced that the patient stayed in treatment. The therapist expressed no concern about the overall effect his methods had on this very troubled patient's feelings about herself, the therapist, and psychotherapy. The therapist was probably unconsciously reinforcing earlier self-object traumas, further damaging the patient's self structure. All this was done with the patient's "best interest" in mind, of course. One wonders how this patient will ever end treatment. It is likely that termination will be directed by the therapist based on his needs. He has clearly demonstrated to the patient that it is the practitioner who controls the treatment. This reinforces the client's dependency—and possibly the therapist's dependence on the patient.

Although the respondents in my study adhered to a wide range of theoretical orientations, most indicated that eclectic, psychodynamic, and specifically psychoanalytic theory is their primary theoretical influence. A smaller percentage considered themselves predominantly nonpsychodynamic. These included client-centered, Gestalt, and humanistic/existential. In all of these, there was no clear or specific difference in terms of the criteria for termination that they actually used. A psychodynamic practitioner was as likely to use the same or very similar criteria as a nonpsychodynamic therapist; that is, the various categories were used with similar frequency by each theoretical school of thought. This is consistent with the discussion in Chapter One of how the different theories of psychotherapy approach the termination process. For instance, the differences between a classical analytic perspective and a self psychology analytic one can be understood as the former looking for conflict resolution and taming of instinctual drives, and the latter dealing with structure building manifested by the emergence of a cohesive self structure.

All psychodynamic theories share a common denominator in that they base "readiness" for termination upon intrapsychic change, which is difficult to observe or quantify. General observations, such as "the patient was able to function better in all areas of life," or the Freudian axiom of the capacity or ability to "work and love" in a more efficacious manner, or improved ability to form lasting relationships did not appear in the research to be tied exclusively to any specific school of thought. This appears to be true in the majority of real-life clinical situations in open-ended psychotherapy. My patients generally report "feeling better" about themselves, "less depressed," "not so worried and nervous anymore," "no more headaches," and "getting along more comfortably with others." Since I strongly believe in a psychology of the self, I am likely to interpret the patient's change as the development of a cohesive self or a more proactive and self-directed personality organization. These questions are irrelevant to the client who only desires to feel better and function better. It is most important not to confuse termination criteria with the complex issue of what variables enhance or cause people to change, heal, and grow.

The manner in which a therapist structures a treatment (usually determined by his or her school of thought and individual style), may be of major importance for that person's understanding of the termination process, including the criteria for termination. A general philosophy that is respectful of patients, and sees them as autonomous, proactive, and self-directive, is essential if the therapist is to facilitate healthy, productive endings. The ability to be empathic, tolerant, and non-manipulative are crucial attributes for which all therapists should strive. Many of the teachings of the self psychology school and the client-centered approach exemplify this philosophy. In their similarities as well as in their differences, these theories support and enhance growth and self-development.

Are Termination Criteria Relevant?

Termination criteria may be more a point of intellectual pursuit for therapists than an actual pathway on which clients can leave treatment. As seen from the literature review, criteria for termination vary greatly. Even within the same school of thought, there are differences of opinion. I propose that the whole idea of criteria may be irrelevant and possibly even damaging to therapy itself. It is likely that all abstract and theoretical discussions of termination criteria are of little value and perhaps actually contribute to practitioners' and patients' confusion about the process of ending treatment. The notion that the therapist determines the guidelines for ending a treatment relationship emphasizes the primacy of the practitioner as the permission-giver. It elevates therapists to the role of controlling authority figures who anoint patients with their blessing or withhold it from them. Such clinicians may set goals according to their belief systems rather than the needs of the patient. When the therapist makes the judgment without the patient's concurrence that it is the right time to stop treatment, the patient is left with numerous unresolved issues. Moreover, the patient must grapple with the fact that he or she was not allowed to participate in the monumental decision to end the therapy. Raskin and Rogers (1989), discussing their treatment philosophy, write: "Clients can be trusted to select their own therapists, to choose the frequency and length of their therapy, to talk or to be silent, to decide what needs to be explored, to achieve their own insights, and to be the architects of their own lives" (p. 156).

The best scenario is the one in which the client is encouraged to initiate the end of therapy, just as he or she initiated its onset. Clinicians must do their best to agree, even though their own personal or theoretical criteria may not have been met. For example, Dr. John T., a practitioner with a self psychology orientation, was treating Ruth N., a nursing student in her mid twenties. This clinician believes that the major criterion for termination of treatment is the formation of a cohesive and structurally complete self. After approximately two years of twice-a-week psychotherapy, the patient was feeling greatly improved, meaning she had a better sense of self, enhanced interpersonal relationships, and a general feeling of contentment and well-being. She was ready to end therapy.

What if Dr. T. had decided that Ms. N.'s self was not structurally complete enough—in his own subjective view—to stop the sessions? Philosophically, this would be consistent because he would be adhering to both his theoretical perspective and the termination criteria generated by the self psychology school of thought. If he disagrees with the patient's decision, based on self psychology ending criteria or any other ending criteria, he places abstract theory above the client's needs and wishes. Therefore, it seems in this not uncommon case that Dr. T.'s termination criteria are not pertinent for practical decision making. In fact, his use of criteria may reinforce countertransference issues, such as his quest for a perfectionistic and perhaps unobtainable psychotherapy outcome, or his inability to let patients go out on their own. As it happened, Dr. T. cared more about his patient than his theory, and he facilitated a successful termination based on his client's needs rather than his own. Respect for patients' will to achieve independence should transcend all theories.

Although termination criteria may be superfluous at best and damaging at worst, there is some value in studying them. A list of ending criteria can be most useful to a practitioner who is trying to understand the "curative" or healing aspect of psychotherapy. Particularly useful are the variables with which practitioners are most comfortable when a client ends treatment.

4

Endings with Very Fragile Individuals

A large number of individuals seen in outpatient, open-ended treatment today have severe psychopathology resulting in extremely fragile and vulnerable personalities. These troubled people with pathological narcissism or borderline syndrome are among the most difficult patients to treat and terminate. It makes both clinical and common sense that the earlier, more intense, and more repetitious the psychic trauma, the more severe the adult psychopathology generally will be. It also follows that the meaning of separation, autonomy, and endings have special significance to these individuals. They represent significant constant challenges and call upon practitioners to continually examine concepts and techniques as well as their own selves.

Understanding the meaning of termination for especially vulnerable patients requires great empathy, creativity, and fortitude. A fictional account is used here to illustrate how carefully clinicians must work to ensure a positive treatment ending for these fragile people. The fictional example, from Judith Rossner's *August* (1983), is included here because it is one of the best illustrations I have ever seen of the many nuances of treatment and of the termination process, whether in life or in literature. And as Rossner says in her author's note, "It would be useful to remember that the psychoanalysis that takes place within this novel bears approximately the resemblance to a real analysis that the novel bears to life."

Two Terminations in *August*

The main client character in Judith Rossner's *August* exhibits many symptoms of pathological narcissism and/or borderline personality, and an exceptional effort is made by the main therapist character to treat her. Much can be understood from the interaction between the very appealing main characters, Dawn Henley, the patient, and her current therapist, Dr. Lulu Shinefeld. However, Dawn's former therapist, Dr. Leif Seaver, is equally significant for this examination of the termination phase. A great deal can be gleaned from a comparison of the two treatments.

Dawn entered treatment the first time, with Dr. Seaver, at the request of her adopted mother after a near-fatal car accident. The acute precipitant for coming to treatment a second time, with Dr. Shinefeld, was again an unconscious suicide gesture, falling asleep at the wheel. When Dr. Shinefeld queries Dawn about her recent accident, Dawn replies, " 'Because he left me.' " Dr. Shinefeld asks, " 'You finished the analysis?' 'He thought I was finished. I was sort of okay. He didn't understand I could only do all the things I was doing because I had him.' 'Did you tell him that?' 'I tried to, but I must've not said it right because I can't believe he would have done it if I had' " (p. 4). This is a clear example of low self-esteem. The patient blames herself rather than another, especially the idealized male therapist.

This termination of Dawn's first course of therapy seems to be initiated by the therapist and is probably the consequence of countertransference issues. It appears that the therapist was so focused on his own agenda that he was out of touch with the patient. Although this insensitivity to Dawn's psychic life could have been limited to the ending phase, we may surmise that Seaver's personality and technique caused him to lack empathy and deep understanding throughout the course of treatment. It is likely that such a therapist might be afraid of being attracted to such a young, lovely, and impressionable woman. He might have feelings about her tremendous dependency upon him. Since these countertransference issues are normal and understandable, a therapist in Seaver's position might choose to work on them through self-analysis or consultation rather than to terminate the relationship as Seaver did. Rossner's fictional foil is well drawn. The countertransference termination he precipitates is typical of real case examples described throughout this book.

A brief look at Dawn's history will reveal how important the issue of ending treatment was for this fictional character. The lesson here holds true as well for real patients with similar characterological makeups. The reader learns that Dawn's mother took her own life when the patient was only six months old, and one year later her father died in a boating accident. Dawn had no recollection of her mother or father. She was raised by unorthodox parents, two lesbians. Dawn's first suicidal gesture was related to their divorce. "Dawn supposed the most important thing to say about Vera and Tony was that for all she'd learned of their problems, she adored them both and felt they'd given her much more than average parents gave their children, in time alone" (p. 6).

The major therapeutic issue here is not that Dawn was reared by a nontraditional couple; it is her exposure to incredible multiple traumas in the form of loss. An astute clinician—of any theoretical orientation—should note not only the impact this had to have on her personality development but also the special meaning endings must have for her. To each patient, termination means something different; it is an error to conceptualize the meaning of ending treatment according to one fixed theory. Through empathy, therapists can learn the unique meaning that termination has for each person. Dawn, and patients with similar histories, symptoms, and self structures, need to be treated and terminated in a manner that reflects their severe degree of self-deficit and fragility. Dr. Seaver appears to be so wedded to the classical analytic approach that he misunderstands Dawn and the type of "corrective emotional experience" that she needs from a self-object to aid in the building of a nuclear self. Moreover, countertransference issues add to his insensitivity and lack of warmth. His treatment of Dawn is anchored in what Kohut (1984) described as an "experience-distant" approach (p. 186).

In Rossner's story, "August" is the code term for partings since it is the traditional month when analysts in New York City take vacations. The author describes the therapists returning en masse after Labor Day in Dawn's words: " 'When all the analysts come back to New York and give birth to their patients' " (p. 10). Because it is obvious that Dawn's unresolved feelings about her former therapist are so severe that she makes another suicide gesture, Dr. Shinefeld asks, " 'Have you considered seeing Dr. Seaver again—rather than another analyst? Or at least talking to him before you see someone else?' " Dawn replies: " 'When I came back from Europe three weeks ago . . . I called and said I needed to talk to him. He said it was too soon and I guess I pleaded with him but . . . . Anyway, I called again last week, after the accident, and when I told him, he said he'd see me. . . .' " (p. 11). Dawn's adopted mother perceptively suggested that maybe seeing another therapist, a woman, would be more helpful. Dawn agreed but felt that " 'first I needed him to know what had happened to me.' "

> I'd brought the print [a piece of Dawn's artwork that held great significance for her]. Not to give him. I just needed him to see the message. The words were very important. I showed it to him, thinking of all the times we'd argued about it, and I kept waiting for the light to go on [to be affirmed and understood]. He was finally going to understand this terribly important thing and explain it to me, and then I'd feel better. Instead he said, *Nice work, Dawn. You're doing some really nice work. Keep it up.* He didn't even remember the arguments! I felt as though I had no importance to him at all, and never had. I was less than a patient, I wasn't even a person! [p. 12]

Dawn's self-injuries are such that Dr. Seaver's communications were far from helpful; instead, they reinforced her feelings of worthlessness. This goes well beyond the normal breaks in empathy that are present throughout the course of all treatments and that in fact help patients grow and mature. Aspects of this fictional treatment could be described as incompetent. Dawn's awareness of Dr. Seaver's limitations, seductions, and lack of empathy become apparent, as do Dr. Shinefeld's empathic grasp of the situation and her ability to convey this to Dawn. "She paused, trying to get over the words. '. . . that since he knew me already, if I came to him the work would go much faster.' Her voice trembled and her lips twisted so she wouldn't cry. 'And that was the end for you,' " affirms the therapist (p. 12). From this painful treatment experience—especially the termination process, which in many ways recapitulated her early losses—Dawn was able to be the one doing the leaving for the first time in her life—and for a healthy reason.

The essence of Dawn's difficulties as they relate to loss and the negligence shown by Dr. Seaver are made very clear as Dr. Shinefeld asks her about the words at the bottom of the lithograph. " 'Dylan Thomas,' Dawn said. 'After the first death there is no other' " (p. 13). Not only does this quote bespeak Dawn's major problem area but perhaps it reflects that of many troubled and characterologically flawed clients. If the concepts of sex and neurosis represent Freud's times and writings, then separation, loss, and characterological deficits may denote our modern society's sterility and mobility. Moreover, the fear of losing one's self runs throughout all human interaction and is an especially charged theme in psychotherapies with patients such as Dawn. They continually struggle with concurrent fears of abandonment and annihilation by a powerful self-object. Clinicians who work with such a population need to be extraordinarily patient, caring, and empathic. Dr. Leif Seaver can be used as a negative role model (the ironic pun on his name is intended).

Dawn personifies the patient who has difficulty engaging because of fears of abandonment. Dr. Shinefeld, who notes Dawn's concerns regarding the clinician's health and empathically connects them to her fear of being rejected, tells the fragile and guarded young woman, " 'There is one promise I can make to you. That I don't ask you to leave here until you're ready. In other words, you can be the one to decide when you're finished.' " (p. 17). Thus she reassures Dawn early in treatment that she comprehends the significance endings have for her, and that in contrast to her first treatment experience, this time Dawn will be allowed to initiate the end of therapy at her own pace.

" 'But what if I finish,' " Dawn asks anxiously, " 'and I leave and then a week or a month or day later something terrible happens to me? Something I have to talk to you about?' 'Well, in that case you'd call me up and come back and we'd talk about it' " (p. 17). Here the therapist introduces the notion of an open-door policy. In contrast, Dr. Seaver's door was closed to Dawn, literally and figuratively. It seems to signify his lack of empathic understanding and, perhaps, his inadequate conceptualization of his patient's psychopathology. In the book, Dr. Shinefeld observes that Dr. Seaver's classical analytic theories distorted his view of the patient, and I agree with that judgment. In real life, this sort of distortion can be characterized as myopia. It is the result of a clinician observing each unique individual through one conceptual lens and dogmatically adhering to theory. Actually, Dawn's emotional conflicts can be understood more clearly when viewed through a self psychology framework or in terms of object relations theory. Rossner describes so aptly Dr. Shinefeld's belief about Dr. Seaver "that like a number of other analysts, he had a deep resistance to exploring that period of life before the relatively comfortable and specific Oedipal attachment began. This was the most difficult and frightening period of life for the obvious reason that words did not exist that were adequate to describe the overpowering feelings engendered in an infant who did not yet have words to describe and sort out those feelings" (p. 26). Since Dawn's problems originated in this preverbal period, a classical analytic approach would be likely to fail. Thus Dr. Seaver failed

Dawn throughout treatment, especially during the termination phase, because his theory that did not match her illness and because he fell short in empathy and genuine human warmth.

Intuitively, because of their own personalities, some classical analysts do practice a less classical form of treatment. Even Dr. Seaver had his moments. Dawn reports that he "was the first one who saw that there were pieces that had to be put together" (p. 52), the pieces being a metaphor for the patient's fragmented nuclear self. "But, then he stopped seeing and they began to come apart." When her therapist initiates this premature, countertransference-ridden termination, Dawn must face the limitations of her savior and the realization that her worst fears—abandonment and rejection—are becoming actualized.

With the help of Dr. Shinefeld, Dawn learns that this termination was not her fault, a fear that is a typical response to these types of iatrogenic endings. She finds the courage to ask a question that clearly reflects her progress: " 'Do you think Dr. Seaver made a mistake with me?' 'Yes,' the doctor said after a considerable length of time. 'I don't know the circumstances that led to the mistake, and I'm uneasy about saying it for that reason. But it seems fairly clear, at least in retrospect, that it was a mistake to terminate your analysis when he did. As he did' " (p. 61). Although the therapist is uncomfortable, she places Dawn's needs above her own, above Dr. Seaver's, above dogmatic theory, and above professional fraternalism.

The fictional Dawn and the majority of clients who have profound personality disturbances, whether narcissistic or borderline, suffer from deficits in their self structure. Dawn speaks of her "nonself" when referring to who she is. Bouncing from poles of aloofness to desperate dependency, the fear of abandonment is ever present. The clinician's departure for vacation in August—or any other break in the empathic connection—stirs up the client's terror of annihilation. Many such patients terminate treatment when faced with such real or perceived partings.

Dawn illuminates this struggle during a session before Dr. Shinefeld is to leave for a holiday. The practitioner gives her a private number to use for emergencies. Dawn stands up to put the folded paper in her pocket, "and when she had finished, she didn't sit down again. 'If you don't mind,' she said, 'I think I'm going to leave now.' 'Are you certain that's what you want to do?' 'Yes,' Dawn said. 'Quite certain.' " Dawn's replies are distant and somewhat sarcastic. She is preparing for the loss. Dr. Shinefeld says, after it is agreed that they will resume sessions in the fall, " 'If you should change your mind and come this week, I'll be here' " (p. 79). Dr. Shinefeld's empathy, skill, and patience lead to a continuation of treatment rather than a "premature" termination.

Dawn returns to treatment, and Dr. Shinefeld now must achieve something nearly impossible, something most clinicians only strive for—complete understanding of the other, total empathy, a response that is free of countertransference. Rossner's therapist comprehends her patient's feelings, reflects them, and lets the patient know she cares. She does not prevent Dawn from leaving, but she also does not give the message that treatment should stop: " 'Well, after all, you're talking about leaving treatment with me. You should know, if you don't already, that I care about you and don't want you to do that—although it's certainly your privilege to leave when you choose' " (p. 109). As Kohut reminds us, confrontation has little value in treatment and patients need their defenses or compensatory structures.

As her treatment and life proceed, Dawn must decide whether to move to Boston with her boyfriend, which would mean changing colleges as well as leaving New York and Dr. Shinefeld. It is important to note the absence of manipulation on the part of the therapist at this juncture. Many clinicians might be tempted to persuade the patient that continuing therapy is crucial and thus encourage the patient to stay close geographically. Such "well meaning" communication is exactly what frightens this type of patient into flight to avoid being taken over. Appropriate response in these situations is like walking a tightrope; leaning just a bit toward either direction can and frequently does end treatment in a negative manner.

In the last sessions, Dawn avoids subjects that would seem of obvious import to any astute practitioner. Again, Rossner has Dr. Shinefeld show outstanding judgment in her restraint from confronting Dawn with matters that would be of greater benefit to the therapist than the patient. "She cut short her last session because she had so much to do before leaving the city. Standing up quite abruptly in the middle of a bland monologue about the difference in climate between Boston and New York, she went to the doctor's chair, leaned over to briskly kiss the top of her head, and pronounced herself grateful for all the doctor had done in enabling her to start a new life. Then, before the doctor had time to collect herself and make some appropriate reply and affectionate farewell, Dawn was out of the room, the door closed behind her" (p. 193). We are not told about Dr. Shinefeld feels on this occasion, but if we project a bit, we might guess at a combination of shock, disappointment, and sadness.

During the first week in August, Dr. Shinefeld opens a package to find a painting from Dawn that reflects the treatment relationship. She writes a thank-you note and in it mentions her anticipation of Dawn returning to therapy in the fall. As the book continues, Dawn's growth and acquisition of a more cohesive self is evident. She comments that she wanted to show one of her earlier works of art to friends and realizes "I'd never brought it home . . . I guess it was somewhere in the back of my mind, but suddenly it seemed wild that I'd left it here all these years. You have it, don't you?' 'In the closet.' 'Do you mind if I take it home?' 'Not if that's what you want to do' " (p. 329).

At the next session, Dawn is angry because she realizes the symbolic meaning of the previous event. " 'You let me just do it' " (p. 330). For the first time in five years, it strikes Dawn that she did not leave a part of herself with the therapist. This is frightening because it reminds her of the disconnection and independence that she desires and fears simultaneously. " 'You really looked at them, you let me leave them here, and they turned out to be very important. My earliest life. The pukey little baby Dr. Seaver didn't want to know. You took her in . . . and now I feel as though you're throwing her out' " (p. 330).

Dawn changes second by second and the reader is witness to her ambivalence about the movement that inevitably puts her face to face with giving up her therapist. " 'I don't think I could forgive you if you got me to stay and then I lost him.' 'Got you to stay?' 'If I stayed because I wasn't finished and then I lost him.' 'People don't get finished,' the doctor said. 'They're not books or statues. . . . The important work of an analysis can be more or less finished, but even that has to be continued by you when you leave. Life isn't a problem that gets solved. In the best analysis every question isn't answered, every difficulty doesn't disappear' " (p. 331).

This important dialogue captures the complex process of ending treatment. Although what the practitioner says is more or less true, in this instance even the empathic, tuned-in Dr. Shinefeld misses Dawn's pressing feelings as they relate to her basic problems and conflicts. " 'Then how will I know when to leave? I can't imagine going unless I'm pulled away. Aside from Jack . . . it seems I could keep on forever' " (p. 331). This dialogue underlines the importance of discussing in a straightforward manner—at the beginning of the therapeutic relationship as well as during it—that therapy is not a fixed state but a process. I share Dawn's concerns, especially for patients with severe characterological problems such as hers.

Dawn continues expressing her ambivalence about staying or going and comes to understand that her identity and sense of self are more important than what city she lives in. Her quandary, although milder and healthier in form, is, as it has always been, about partings. She feels, as many other patients do, that her growth and her more cohesive self are tied to the therapist. " 'There are times when I feel quite certain that what I want to do is commute to Washington for weekends until the end of July, then move there . . . And then there are other times when I know that there's no way in the world I'm going to walk out of this office forever and into August' " (p. 338). Clearly, Dr. Shinefeld needs to be cautious and not push too much for Dawn's move. It is easy, at a juncture like this, for a therapist to act out countertransference issues with a patient such as Dawn, who is so needy and dependent.

In May, Dawn makes a firm decision to move to Washington. In the next sessions, a feeling tone of resolution and calmness is dominant. She discusses her feelings of moving on: " 'On the other hand, you have to go to new places and meet new people. From the world of the present' " (p. 347). New places—as opposed to the safety of the past and the known; Dawn—and all of us—must continue to take risks if we are to change and grow.

The healing, empathic, "unconditional positive regard" and love that she received are evident in Dawn's growth. Reminiscing and feeling the warmth of her self-object, she says: "I love you very much, you know . . . I feel as though you love me . . . Not in the same way that you love your own children, but it's real anyway" (p. 352). The fictional Dr. Leif Seaver and all the real Dr. Seavers could never provide the type of therapeutic environment that Dawn and patients like her need to heal and to end treatment in a healthy fashion. It is a two-sided issue of theoretical approach and the clinician's personality. What Dr. Seaver lacks, Dr. Shinefeld has in abundance, and it goes beyond theoretical differences. Warmth, caring, compassion, and kindness are immeasurable and frequently overlooked healing qualities.

In the last weeks of her analysis, Dr. Shinefeld resisted the all-too-tempting posture of trying to manipulate Dawn into staying, which would have subtly infantilized her further as well as exploited her. This young woman continues to grapple with the pain of separating, but a new self is emerging. " 'I guess you don't love me enough to make me stay, is how I feel. Not make me stay. You couldn't do that. But urge me to . . . Well, not urge, because then I'd be scared that you thought I couldn't manage on my own, or that you needed me . . . I don't want you to need me exactly. But I need you

to care about what happens to me. I couldn't bear it if I
thought you would forget me.' 'Do you believe that it's possible that I might?' Dawn cried softly. 'No, not really . . . Even
if I don't think about you all the time . . . That's not the
same as forgetting you' " (pp. 355–356).

In the final session Dawn asks questions of her therapist that many patients would like to ask. " 'What are you
going to do when I leave here?' " (p. 373). In honest and
humanistic terms, not hiding behind theory to defend against
feelings, Dr. Shinefeld replies: " 'I think that probably I'll
come back to my chair and just sit by myself for a while . . .
and think about you. Perhaps I'll open my picture then. . . .
And perhaps I'll cry a little . . .' 'You will?' Dawn asked in a
whisper. 'Perhaps. At least I'll feel what someone referred
to once as a sweet sadness . . . pleasure in the work we've
done . . . regret that I won't be seeing you' " (p. 373).

There is much beauty and honesty in this interchange.
Dr. Shinefeld's self-disclosures allow Dawn to see her as a
human being, which Dawn has begun to do subtly and slowly
over time. She gives Dawn permission to feel the real pain
and excitement of ending—the loss and the surge of joy about
new beginnings.

It struck me once when I was terminating with a long-
term client and not allowing myself a few minutes before the
next patient, that I was not doing the best thing either for the
terminating client, for myself, or for my next patient. This
kind of scheduling does not give the relationship the respect
it deserves and thus diminishes its import. Even if I have to
make schedule changes that affect other clients, it is well
worth it. By not allowing myself those minutes I did not give
myself the time to mourn, celebrate, or feel what I needed to
feel. What Dawn wants to know is what all patients want to
know—what all human beings who feel want to know: How
important am I to you? If after three to fifteen years of being
with a person in a context as intimate as therapy we don't
have feelings or don't take time to acknowledge and understand our feelings, we make a sham of the therapeutic process.
The more authentic we are to our feelings the better, espe-

cially as they relate to stopping treatment. A certain amount of self-disclosure by clinicians is essential throughout all stages of psychotherapy; perhaps there is a correlation between time in treatment and self-disclosures. Certainly, in the final sessions it can only enhance the treatment if the therapist serves as a healthy role model who enables the patient to express feelings about loss, endings, and new beginnings. Dr. Shinefeld offers us an excellent model. This humanistic concept is far removed from the Freudian axiom of the analyst being like a surgeon who maintains distance and neutrality. Somewhere between Freud's surgery and the enmeshment of an overly involved clinician is the appropriate posture.

Rossner's delightful novel ends with perhaps the ultimate characterization of treatment outcome and growth:

> She turned on her desk light to look at the framed oil painting that Dawn had left with her. Done in a more primitive style than the one Dawn usually employed, it showed a young woman emerging from what might have been a subway kiosk in a city whose buildings resembled Washington's. The woman had blond hair and wore a dress in a brilliant print of purple, red, and blue. Painted inside that large woman, so that she constituted a good portion of but not the entire body's interior, was another considerably smaller woman whose small head reached the place where the large one's heart might have been, whose tiny arms fitted into the other's large ones, and so on. The small woman wore a brilliant red dress and had dark hair close to the color of Dr. Shinefeld's [p. 376].

Model for Positive Endings

The fictional situations in *August* illuminate many of the real-life themes discussed here. Rossner's work particularly demonstrates the salient theories and personality characteristics of clinicians that enable positive endings to evolve. Dr.

Shinefeld's empathic, nondirective, and respectful technique results in warm and human interactions and is a model for positive terminations, in contrast to Dr. Seaver's more distant and theoretically dogmatic style, which appears to lack an empathic grasp of the treatment. These two characters represent distinct poles of therapeutic interactions. Certainly, all therapeutic endings are not so touching and poetic, and the more serious the client's psychopathology, the more challenging the termination. However, the same basic principles of empathy, warmth, and respect should guide us, whether our patient is a borderline personality or a highly functioning neurotic.

5

Patients Who Are Therapists: The Experience of Letting Go

Using treatment clients who are therapists themselves as research subjects elicits some interesting and valuable information. A substantial number of the respondents in both my 1982 and 1986 studies had been or still were in treatment. Although the termination experiences of therapist-patients are similar to those of lay clients, patients who are therapists are generally better equipped to understand the process and recognize issues that complicate the ending phase. Being human, they are not better equipped to avoid the emotional fallout of a negative termination, however. Clinician-clients are especially valuable for generating hypotheses and ideas, particularly when qualitative research methodologies are being used to explore and suggest hypotheses, theories, and concepts.

The psychotherapeutic treatment that therapist-patients receive is often the basic form of the treatment model they offer clients. Thus, the manner in which their own treatment ends seems to have a direct influence on the way they handle the terminal phase with their patients. For example, when a treating therapist adheres to the theory of psychological cure and strives for a perfect outcome for the therapist-patient, the latter will tend to seek idealistic outcomes for his or her own patients. This quest for a cure, rather than for change and growth, may be one reason therapists tend to stay a long time in their personal psychotherapy and why the treatments in their own practices are often quite lengthy.

Demonstrating the lack of agreement on the issue of cure versus change, Gaskill (1980) speaks of the varied views "as to the extent and depth of the changes expected while maintaining the achievement of a satisfactory termination" (p. 12). He goes on to say that "one is immediately struck by the trend towards more modest expectations with less emphasis on 'cure' " (p. 12). As noted above, Freud himself initially spoke more modestly about the expectations and goals of psychoanalysis than modern theorists do. Since Freud's time, the treatment process, both analytic and psychodynamic, has moved increasingly toward more perfectionistic outcomes and longer treatment durations. Why this has happened is not clear. It could be a self-serving phenomenon, a form of cognitive dissonance, a reflection of the complexities of today's society, or just the assumption that more is better. Recently, however, there appears to be a welcome trend toward more modest outcome criteria.

When Do They End Treatment?

Interviews with therapist-patients show that they initiate termination of their own treatment almost 100 percent of the time. This appears consonant with the initiation of termination when they were the practitioners working with clients. In general, they report similar termination criteria for their own treatments as they do for their clients. Global improvement factors are the most frequently mentioned. The cost/benefit analysis also occurs in approximately the same proportion for therapists' own treatment experiences and for their lay clients. The therapist-patients referred much less frequently to specific external/observable or intrapsychic factors in deciding to end psychotherapy, and the presence of external factors unrelated to treatment is approximately the same for both groups.

The criterion of the development of a more equal relationship between the two parties has a slightly different cast when the patient is a practitioner rather than a lay person. The therapist-patient has a greater ability to articulate and identify this egalitarian interaction. The gradual change in relationship is important both as a termination criterion and as a cue for signaling the end of treatment. It can be labeled, depending on theoretical underpinnings, as equalization of the relationship, development of more peerlike relationships, or resolution of transference issues.

Being a clinician as well as a client also can create a unique problem in regard to termination. Therapist B. T. reports: "I started to share office space with my therapist and things got confusing. There was an issue of confidentiality which I believe was violated." While this therapist-patient's actual reason for ending treatment is not typical, it is not uncommon for an established clinician to share office space and consultation with therapists who are patients or former patients. Generally, this should not be done because it creates or reinforces a type of enmeshment that is unhealthy for the client and is a variation on the theme of not letting go. Enmeshment and mutual holding-on not only lead to negative treatment endings, they can lead to no ending at all.

Some of the therapist-patients I surveyed stopped therapy because they did not agree with their practitioner's approach to treatment. Therapist G. K. states: "I'm not sure if my therapist and I had a theoretical or personal difference on an issue that came up. He kept on interpreting my feelings and plans as depressive and unhealthy. I disagreed and felt what I wanted to do was somewhat nontraditional but that changing my lifestyle was a positive and very healthy decision." This particular treatment was quite complex and not easily reduced to a concise formula. However, it is very likely that countertransference was a significant factor in the ending. Perhaps more important, the treating therapist was making an intrusive value judgment about his therapist-patient's desire to change her life. Because he failed to stay empathically in tune with her, he precipitated an abrupt termination and lost her. Therapist G. K. might have been able to accept a direct difference of opinion, even about value judgments; it appears that what was unacceptable to her as a patient was the clinician's lack of true empathy as well as his criticism of her plans. A lay client might have sensed this lack, but probably would not have recognized it as a "theoretical difference."

It is clear from the data about practitioners' own treatments that countertransference issues are prevalent in all types of therapy. Therapist P. B., a humanistic, client-centered practitioner in treatment with a similar type of clinician, comments: "I felt I was not getting enough out of the sessions. I brought up termination and the therapist said that he wanted to make the experience a mutually satisfying one." Although the treating therapist could be given some credit for his directness, he should not have interjected his own needs into the treatment. A basic treatment tenet must be to minimize the therapist's needs and provide an atmosphere conducive to the patient's growth, whatever one's theoretical approach.

Satisfactory Versus Unsatisfactory Progress

Decrease in presenting problems is a criterion that is reported in approximately equal proportions by professional and nonprofessional patients. Therapist M. F. states: "The conflicts and issues that brought me to treatment were greatly improved. I saw a light at the end of the tunnel. The pain was there at times, but less intense and less overwhelming. My initial difficulties were improved to the point where I was comfortable." Like other therapist-patients, when she felt that her progress had reached a satisfactory plateau, this practitioner initiated the end of treatment and her therapist agreed.

However, another group of therapist-patients reported ending treatment because their progress was not satisfactory. The fact that there are more professional patients than lay patients in this category may be because therapists are more knowledgeable and therefore more sophisticated and critical about the treatment relationship. A subcategory here is one of therapist-patients who felt as if they were "getting worse" in treatment. This feeling is somewhat different from not being satisfied or sensing that one is not making progress, and patients who are not therapists also experience it. How the treating therapist handles such situations is most important. Therapist L. P. reports: "My treatment was psychoanalytic, meeting four times a week for four years. I brought up terminating and told him that treatment at this point was making me sicker. He told me I was not ready to stop treatment and that I would be sorry. He said I would be back because I was not finished. This made me feel very angry, but also extremely scared and frightened."

The therapist-patient did end the treatment in spite of her fears. The inappropriate and hostile countertransference-ridden remarks of the therapist speak for themselves. This particular termination probably reflects early- and middle-phase treatment problems that were not processed properly by the treating therapist. Moreover, it confirms my belief that people know best what they need.

Therapist L. P. and therapist M. F. had very different treatments and terminations. One was productive, almost ideal; the other was negative and counterproductive. Seven years after terminating her iatrogenic treatment, therapist L. P. went back for one session to see her former clinician. "I went because it was unfinished business for me. Also, a part of me wanted to show him I was doing great. After the session I realized I felt depressed. He was a person who focused only on psychopathology, never on a person's strengths or health. When all is said and done, there were parts of the treatment that were helpful. But in retrospect, I think I wasted a lot of time and money. I could have made those gains with another therapist and maybe a different approach in six months to a year."

In contrast, because therapist M. F.'s clinician agreed with her decision to end treatment, she had a very good termination experience that she uses as a model when working with her own clients. She initiated termination after reaching

a point where *she* was comfortable. When the treating therapist agreed with her decision to end, therapist M. F. felt
affirmed, valued, and respected. Their empathic connection,
mutual agreement, and collaboration set the tone for a termination that was beneficial to her in a deep and self-enhancing
way, and that benefited her in all areas of her life, including
her professional role. Clients of this therapist-patient are
fortunate.

Therapist M. F. learned how to structure the process of
ending psychotherapy from the model her own therapist used.
Therapist L. P. also learned a great deal about treatment and
termination from her therapist—mostly what not to do. Fortunately, she was resilient enough to find another practitioner
who was a far better self-object and role model.

Termination Experiences

The example of therapist V. S., who was in the process of
terminating a thirteen-year psychoanalytic treatment, offers
some illuminating insights. She says that she had tried to end
the analysis about two years before she finally stopped. "I
tried but it was obviously premature. I set the date thinking
that the limit would force me to deal with issues that were
difficult for me. Two months before the actual date, I started
to feel it was not right for me. I felt frightened—more frightened than I should have been if it was the correct time for me
to terminate." Her treating therapist was relatively neutral
about her decision to end. Unlike many of the previous
examples, he did not interfere with therapist V. S.'s plan and
refrained from passing judgment. Thus she felt understood,
respected, and valued.

Sometimes, however, leaving too many decisions to the
patient can be almost as nonproductive as being overly directive. For example, another therapist-patient reports that his
practitioner said he should come for treatment as long as he
was getting something out of it. "When I felt I had reached
the limit of the usefulness of the experience and brought this
up, asking his opinion, he said, 'What do *you* think?' I did

not find this very helpful." In this case, the treating therapist seemed to be using a technique that, planned or unplanned, is counterproductive to a positive ending outcome. It is an extreme form of neutrality that can be dehumanizing. It is a form of withholding, even hostility. The essential empathy and connectiveness were missing in the treating therapist's use of questions to answer questions. Often in such situations, countertransference issues, whether conscious or unconscious, have caused the clinician to resort to this technique as a type of code to express nonsupport of the termination. As this termination proceeded, although it was not acknowledged as such, the polarization between the two continued. The client reported: "I felt my therapist was very unhelpful and my frustration grew. I felt alone." It became clear that if this therapist-patient was ever going to leave treatment, he would have to do it on his own.

For therapist V. S., however, her clinician's neutrality was a positive factor in her termination. She did not need to rebel in order to prove she was an autonomous adult. Her therapist's neutral calm enabled her to look within herself, examine her own feelings, and act accordingly. "This time it feels right—less frightening. In some ways, it's sort of a lift." In this, she touched on a common theme in termination, although it is seldom discussed by those who write about the ending process: the excitement of accomplishment, the exhilaration of growth and movement, and the resonance of new beginnings.

She describes the process as gradual. "I asked him what he thought of setting a date for one year. He felt we should concentrate for the first six months on finishing up the therapeutic work still to be done, and then take six months to talk about termination." The treating therapist is offering some structure as to how the process should unfold. Whether one agrees with the specifics or not, it is apparent that the philosophical and practical aspects are quite good. Immersed in the ending process, in the interview the therapist-patient anticipated the loss of this incredibly important relationship. "I've noticed of late even saying goodbye to acquaintances has been very painful." She was working through her feelings and preparing herself for departure of a self-object who had been immensely helpful and important to her. However, while wondering about the ending of treatment, therapist V. S. also feared that it would not end. "I'm concerned that a number of friends have terminated their treatments [analysis] and had to go back two or three times. I hope this doesn't happen to me. How do you know? It concerns me. I guess there are no concrete gauges."

Therapist C. P. reported that after approximately two years of once-a-week psychoanalytically oriented psychotherapy, his practitioner suggested that they look at the direction the therapy was taking. "I felt in total agreement about looking at where I was headed. There was an interface of many things including money, defenses, resistances, and goals." Here the therapist-patient is struggling with the cost/benefit ratio just as any other psychotherapy consumer. What is unusual is that the treating therapist initiated the discussion. She did not directly suggest termination; she only intended to explore it as a possibility. This can be a desirable and helpful technique if it is conducted empathically, timed appropriately, and geared toward the well-being of the clinician-client. From the interview it is clear that this discussion of the treatment process did not evolve from countertransference issues within the treating therapist.

Therapist C. P. continues with his story: "It came down to two choices: go into analysis [the treating practitioner was an analyst who was providing psychotherapy to the therapist-patient] or terminate, knowing I had done some very good and productive work. My therapist felt that if I chose to continue treatment, I should consider more intensive treatment. He was correct and I believed him. I decided to end. We took about four months. I might have gone on indefinitely. It was comfortable."

This junction is important to explore. Here is a typical open-ended, out-patient, private practice, once-a-week treatment that has been productive for the patient, a clinician himself. The exemplary aspects of this case are the nice manner in which the treating therapist broached the issue of the direction of treatment and the way they agreed on a resolution. This could have been a case where the therapist used the rationalization of "respecting the patient's autonomy" to thus let treatment drift on and on until it evolved into a negative termination. The therapist-patient understandably could have begun to feel held onto. This, of course, is the opposite of encouraging independence, autonomy, and self-development.

The other alternative is what therapist C. P. worried about, "going on indefinitely." Perhaps too many open-ended psychotherapies end up in this category. Treatment becomes a nice chatty relationship with both people avoiding the issue of parting. (It is true that there are some interminable patients who are in need of a self-object to maintain basic daily living functions. There is nothing unethical about seeing such people week in and week out. Helping them stay working, keeping their few relationships going, or keeping them out of the hospital are commendable goals. Such clients, however, are not the subject here.)

Although he felt "appropriate anxiety" about ending treatment, therapist C. P. handled it well. "I felt and still do feel good about the treatment." After two years, he entered psychoanalysis with another clinician. "I was afraid of analysis lasting forever," he reports. "I know many people who have been in twelve to eighteen years, and some are still going. The analyst assured me an analysis that lasts that long is an analytic failure and this comforted me." When asked how he thought this current treatment might end and who would initiate it, therapist C. P. replied, "Who knows? Theory says it will become apparent." He would know within himself, he said, through his "analyzing ego." "I'll be able to make sense of my own experience and be fully aware of my world, including my affective life, feeling things more fully. My self-esteem will be very good and my problems will be all worked through." He seems to have lost his fears of treatment length and become a direct participant in a system that develops perfectionistic and unobtainable outcome expectations.

The irony is that therapist C. P. may become one of the people who caused him concern—an interminable patient. However, he is aware of the importance of the termination process. "I don't terminate [my own patients] in a planned, meaningful way enough, and I want to improve in this area. My first treatment ended in a planned way and that really helped me. I guess I should remember that and use *that* as a model more."

A positive termination experience should not be a matter of luck, as therapist R. J. felt hers was because she knew many colleagues who had had "bad experiences." If more treating therapists had as much knowledge about the ending phase as they do about the beginning and middle stages, both therapist-patients and lay clients would leave treatment feeling good about their therapists, about the psychotherapeutic process, and about themselves. Even more important, when therapists are "lucky" enough to have positive terminations in their personal treatment, these good experiences serve as models for the ending phase in their own practices.

An Interview with a Therapist-Patient

Following is an interview conducted with Kate W., a psychodynamic practitioner who had some interesting and illuminating comments to make about her personal termination experience.

SK: What brought you into treatment?

KW: My life was a bit chaotic, I would say. I was involved in many professional endeavors—teaching, postgraduate training—and not doing well in any of them. I think, in general, I was just depressed and that's why so many aspects of my life were not going well.

SK: What was the orientation of the treatment?

KW: I started in psychodynamic psychotherapy and ended up in analysis.

SK: For how long?

KW: Six years. I was in psychotherapy once a week for about a year, and then I went in for twice-a-week treatment. Then I started analysis and stayed in that a little more than three years.

SK: A lot of people start out going more frequently and then taper. Your process was reversed, mostly because of the transition from psychotherapy to analysis.

KW: Right. I think I probably really did need to go more often than once a week. One of the things were some rather fixed patterns I had of relating to people. The psychiatrist felt that analytic treatment would be best to get at the root of those patterns.

SK: How would you rate the treatment in terms of help-fulness?

KW: I've had different views of it at different times. When I was going through it, I felt it was extremely helpful. In retro-spect, after being out of treatment now for four months, I feel it's more in the moderately helpful range. I did feel I was able to understand myself a lot better and understand some pat-terns that had gotten me into trouble before. Because I had been in treatment before, I felt like I got a handle on that. I got myself out of the jams I was in and got a sense of what acting out really represented for me. I could say to myself, if you start getting into trouble, it's because you're not feeling good about something. So I thought it was very helpful.

SK: Can you tell me a little about the process of ending? Who initiated it, for example?

KW: I think it was over a rather extended period of time. Initially I wasn't even sure that it was really what I was saying or indicating to him. But I recall that last summer I made the statement: "I'm not even sure what I'm coming here for." I probably could have gone a lot longer. The major precipitant triggering my decision was his decision to raise fees, and he did it in a rather, I thought, precipitous fashion. In some ways, I feel like I'm putting it all on him, but I'll tell the other side of it.

SK: How long had you been thinking about it?

KW: When I made that initial statement about not being sure what I was coming for any more, it was three months before the raise issue came up. So some of it was sort of on my mind. When he decided to raise fees, at that point I think I considered it more seriously because the increase in fees bothered me. It wasn't just that; at that point, I started re-evaluating.

SK: How did you experience the raise in fees?

KW: I was angry about it. I was angry because fees had been raised before and I had reacted the first time more strongly. But this time, I felt like it didn't make a lot of sense to raise my fee, given that I was coming in four times a week. The fee was already high, especially for a person who had no insurance. I was paying out of pocket. And, of course, all these things were factors he knew. So he seemed insensitive. Sort of, like, he's going to make this decision. I really protested, so he backed off and the fee was never increased, so it wasn't actually the money.

What I really started asking myself was, "What am I going for?" And then, as I thought about it very carefully, I kind of felt like I could go on in treatment forever. I could always find something to talk about. And I decided that I was really interested in being more autonomous, which had already been an issue for me for a long time, being the youngest in the family. I felt like so many things were in place and the other things that remained as issues I could resolve myself. So I told him I was going to terminate.

SK: So you clearly initiated it, brought it up first.

KW: Yes, I did.

SK: Do you think he understood what it meant to you? Do you think that's why he backed down? Did he ever really talk about the fees? Understand what you were feeling about the issue?

KW: He understood the issue of the fees. Had I remained in treatment he would have allowed me to decide when the fee was going to be increased. And I talked to him about the fact that I was already paying mine out of pocket and I was coming in four times a week and that kind of thing. He seemed to have some awareness of it, that he acknowledged. Based on how it was brought to me initially, I thought he was paying lip service to understanding my position as opposed to really understanding what I was saying and feeling.

SK: That's what I was picking up from you while we were talking. It sounds as if you felt a lack of empathic understanding about the fee issue but he thought he should back off a bit.

KW: Right. He thought he should, for the sake of keeping the treatment alive. So that part he didn't understand and then he never really acknowledged what I was saying about the meaning of the raise and the timing—he just pooh-poohed the whole thing. It was like he was saying, "All of a sudden you want to stop treatment. That doesn't make any sense." I felt that as a real narcissistic injury. It didn't make sense that he wouldn't understand my feelings.

SK: Mostly you just needed him to understand, not necessarily agree with your position.

KW: Yes! And then, I was thinking about this recently, the thing he ended up doing was to ask me what I thought the real reasons were, and I went over them. I told him about being sixteen years old and asking an older sister to make waffles for me. She said, "If you want waffles, make them yourself." It wasn't till that point that I really decided I could cook and I did. I said, "I could come here forever, you know, and I've got to be on my own." I thought he never really understood or acknowledged that part.

A couple of weeks later, he told me he thought the real

reason I wanted to end had to do with wanting to find a marriage partner. And since I found one, I was terminating treatment. At the time, I laughed; it sounded kind of funny. Because, of course, that was one of the things that had been on my mind for a very long time. But that wasn't the reason I came into treatment. And I don't think that was the reason I wanted to leave treatment. So again, it sort of felt like a slap.

SK: He didn't quite get what you were feeling?

KW: No, he didn't. He definitely didn't.

SK: It was an interpretation that missed.

KW: It not only missed, I almost felt it later to be kind of hostile to me. At the time I didn't.

SK: It sounds like your therapist was having a lot of feelings about your ending treatment—perhaps some countertransference feelings.

KW: Yes, that's what I got. So it wasn't an ideal termination, although it wasn't a bad one. I felt like I was able to express what things were on my mind. It wasn't too bad.

SK: What would have been a better termination experience for you, if you could go back and do it over?

KW: What would have been helpful initially, I think, when I got past the issues or crises and trauma, was to talk about ending treatment. If he had acknowledged that, perhaps we could have begun to think about a termination, or when I really started talking about it, if he had agreed or at least understood. I remember now—I left this out when I was telling you before—he said because I was tearful when we talked about termination, that I really did not want to terminate, that my tears were an indication that I really didn't want to leave. At first that sort of threw me, and then I was talking to someone about it and they said, "You know, that doesn't really make sense because you had a good treatment experience." So I really felt like he was trying to hold me back.

Then instead of just sort of working out what his issues were, and saying okay, let's begin the process of termination, it was more like he conveyed an attitude, "I'm not going to do anything to interfere." Well, by this attitude, he was interfering because it was clear there was something else on his mind, that he would like to keep me there. So I found that difficult.

Then I think the other thing was, toward the end just before I was leaving, he made an interpretation like, "Well, it's kind of like watching a two-year-old who's just learning to walk. Like you're apprehensive, you don't want to hold out your hand to keep them from falling, you want them to do it on their own. You don't really know what's going to happen so you're feeling sort of anxious about the process." I recall that I became very silent, and he asked what I was thinking about? And I told him, "You know, I'm not a two-year-old. I'm an adult. It's entirely different." He said, "Well, no analogy matches." Well, that one really fell short! So I felt he wanted to hold on.

SK: It certainly sounds like countertransference issues. He has an excellent reputation of being a good therapist, one of the best. Very skilled, very empathic. But it seems you're saying when it came to termination, he sort of missed the mark.

KW: Yes, clearly.

SK: Perhaps because he had trouble letting go, he couldn't be there for you.

KW: Right. He was assuming I felt two, when in fact I felt like an adult with normal feelings of leaving.

SK: You resented a metaphor of treatment that likened you to a young child, especially when you had grown in treatment so much?

KW: Exactly.

SK: So, to do it better, differently, you really would have wanted him to be more in tune with what you needed, not with what he needed?

KW: Right. I think that would have helped a lot. Particularly because dependency had been a very strong issue for me and I probably could have done analysis for another five or ten years and he wouldn't have blinked an eye. Something else came up that also made me uncomfortable. He told me that he had developed this new procedure for people who were terminating which was for them to come back in a year. I would make the appointment and pay—he made that very clear—then talk about what was helpful and what was not helpful in treatment. He asked me to think about it. I said I did not want to come back for an appointment, especially for me to pay for it. It would be more for him—I know how I'm doing.

SK: For research?

KW: I'm not sure what the purpose was, but I felt it was a bit too intrusive.

SK: Is there anything I haven't asked you that you think might be valuable for people to understand so as professionals we can learn how to end better?

KW: One issue in particular is the maturation process, a rather lengthy one because I talked to him at the beginning of January. I really wanted to terminate within three weeks, given that I was coming in four days a week. He said he didn't think that was advisable. I felt he was warning me, telling me I was doing something wrong, maybe undermining my positive feelings.

SK: His warnings made you feel like you were making a mistake, or you weren't ready?

KW: Or like something terrible would happen. And I question that. Because if I went bankrupt, he wouldn't expect me to come in. It was like, "The best way to do it is for you to continue to come in for two more weeks four times a week, then three times a week for a couple of weeks, then one time a week." It ended up being six weeks. But it was a warning:

"If you don't terminate this way, it's like a diver coming up too soon. Something's going to happen."

SK: You'll get the bends [laughing].

KW: You'll get brain-damaged [laughing]. It was that kind of thing. It scared me. So I followed his advice, but I still question it. What would be helpful, under normal circumstances if the patient is doing fairly well, is for the therapist to express that. And then to leave an open door. But to leave the patient feeling that he's going to be okay and here are the things that lead to the process of us becoming okay, or the things that were worked out.

SK: I think that's one of the bigger mistakes therapists make, too. I believe there's not enough affirmation for health along the way, even in the beginning and the middle, and especially in the end. We're too focused on "unhealth" or looking for pathology.

KW: Right.

SK: What have you felt in the past three or four months since ending?

KW: After the first couple of weeks, I know I was kind of sad, feeling a sense of loss. But interestingly, the thing I felt the most was a tremendous relief and excitement. Because, obviously, coming in four days a week had really compromised my schedule. I was always worried about getting to treatment, wherever I was. It ended up really being a hassle. I felt this enormous relief, like "I don't have to go in and talk, I can take my own counsel or talk to a friend or something." I just really felt great. Sometimes I felt almost giddy with excitement—"I'm not in analysis anymore!" I still feel that. Sometimes I think about how he looks. I imagine what it would be like to run into him on the street. I did see him once, but he was a half a block away. I didn't feel like running over to him, but it was sort of nice to see that he was still out there.

SK: Still around?

KW: That sort of thing, right. Mixed feelings. I think they were really positive feelings about myself as opposed to the way I used to feel. I was kind of wondering if maybe all those years were necessary to accomplish my goals. I try not to dwell on that because it is over. I think it's made me not only a better therapist but a better person. So I try not to think, "Gee, what would it have been like if I had terminated a year ago, or two or three years ago?" But to go on from here and say I did a lot of good things. Now I made this decision and I'm going on and I feel great.

Therapist Kate W.'s own treatment was a generally helpful and positive experience. The precipitant that triggered the end was the issue over fees. The patient experienced the raise as a narcissistic injury. Insult was added to injury when the clinician failed to comprehend the meaning this issue held for her, and there was a break in the empathic bond. Perhaps, as in other cases, the patient used this situation to break away since there are no guidelines or clear theory for this perplexing process. The therapist-patient's feeling that she could go on forever is also a signal that perhaps treatment has outlived its usefulness. Practitioners should not be threatened by such statements; rather, they should rejoice in the success of their hard work.

Kate W. was hurt during the ending process because her normally empathic and intuitive clinician was not tuned in to her during this stage. She perceived his interpretations as infantilizing and his attitude of "I won't interfere" as an interference, a kind of passive, possibly hostile, resistance. In this case, the practitioner seems more anxious than the patient about ending treatment, expressing this with his metaphor of apprehensive parents. His countertransference feelings convey doubts to the patient about her future well-being. However, after terminating, she experiences some appropriate sad feelings but they are overshadowed by her sense of relief, joy, and excitement about new beginnings. It is interesting that the literature is more focused on negative posttreatment cases involving major regressions and loss. I have found most people express feelings of pride and self-enhancement after leaving therapy.

6

How Nontherapist Patients Experience Termination

An investigation into ways to end treatment would be incomplete without contributions from clients who are not clinicians. The following two interviews with layperson clients demonstrate from the patient's perspective how affirming or how devastating the practitioner's attitude can be to the ending of a treatment relationship.

A Positive Termination

Barbara T. had been in treatment with Diane F., a psychodynamic psychotherapist, for over two years. Ms. T. considered her therapy and termination to have been positive, even though she ended it abruptly and defensively. I interviewed her about the issues relating to end of her therapy.

SK: Before we talk about the end, could you tell me a little about what brought you into therapy to begin with?

BT: I was real sad and crying all the time, and every time I'd go into a friend's office, he'd say, "Are you okay?" and I'd say, "Yeah." And finally one day I went in and said, "I'm not okay." He said, "Would you like to talk to somebody?" and I said, "No, I'm not ready to do that." So a couple of weeks later, I said, "I think I'm ready now."

SK: Would you say you were sad and depressed?

BT: Yes, that is why I went in for therapy. Also, I was kind of wondering who the heck I was.

SK: How long were you actually in therapy?

BT: About two, two-and-a-half years.

SK: So a lot of things had been going on for a long time— things were building up, it sounds like. Was there any acute precipitant that brought you in?

BT: No, there wasn't anything really acute and it wasn't any one thing. A lot of it probably had to do with the fact that I saw fairly healthy people who were going to therapy and thought it was a good idea. I knew that I was depressed a lot, although I didn't call it depressed at that time. I was sad a lot. I used to go home from work and fall asleep by six o'clock, then oversleep and be late for work the next day, even though I had plenty of sleep. I knew that I just wasn't right. It got to be worse and worse until I thought maybe some of these people that suggested therapy had a good idea.

SK: So then you got a referral from somebody you worked for. How long did it take you to actually make the phone call?

BT: About two weeks.

SK: How did things go in the beginning?

BT: I didn't know much about therapy, but she was okay to talk with. I never really even thought about whether she was the right person or that we needed to really hit it off or any-thing. It was comfortable that first day. She just asked me a couple of questions and it just took off. I went in once a week.

SK: What was the beginning like?

BT: It was just that I really needed to talk and try to figure out for myself what was making me so sad. At the start it felt like it could go on forever. That's how I felt. That's part of why it ended when it did. I didn't want to do this forever, that was in my mind. I went for two-and-a-half years. I figured that was enough.

SK: So the therapist didn't really talk about ending, either—how you may know when you're ready. It wasn't a question that you asked, either?

BT: There was no conversation about ending in the beginning.

SK: How did the end of your therapy come about? Who initiated it, in terms of talking about it first—issues like that?

BT: Well, I think before I started going out with Kevin I was feeling a lot better and doing a lot of different things. But I was thinking this could go on forever and ever because I feel I could always find something to talk about. I didn't have a lot of people that I really talked to about intimate things. So I knew it would be hard to give up. But I was concerned about the issue of coming in forever and was determined not to be one of those people that would be in therapy or analysis for decades. That kind of thing worried me. I knew people who did that and it didn't make sense to me.

SK: Twelve, fifteen, twenty-five years—I guess we all know people who stay that long.

BT: Yeah, that really seemed kind of weird to me. That sort of started it, I think. I would think, "Do they still need to go once or twice a week even?" I didn't want to be that dependent on this person, you know. It was a concern, but it wasn't like I thought about it often.

SK: Was that theme there a long time before you actually talked about it?

BT: I think so.

SK: It was in the back of your mind somewhere?

BT: Not in the beginning of therapy, but maybe after a year or so. Then I kind of started wondering if it would ever end or if you always went forever. And I didn't want to do that.

SK: So do you remember at what point you actually initiated discussion about it?

BT: I don't think I even really talked to Diane about that aspect of it. I think I didn't start talking about ending until after I got engaged, and at that point I was sure I wanted to stop therapy anyway. That was in January and I ended in March or April. I guess I felt I didn't want to talk about some of the things I was thinking. So I just decided it would be a good time to quit.

SK: Would it be too uncomfortable for you to tell me some of those things? What you're really saying is that a lot of progress took place in the therapy and then you got to a certain place—

BT: No. I can tell you some of my friends were trying to discourage me from being engaged and getting married at that time. I was getting angry at them and starting to question why, without even having met my fiancé, they were so negative about it. One day I told a special friend, someone I looked up to and respected, about my engagement and he was not very happy for me. Instead, he encouraged me to take my time and be more sure because everything seemed to be happening so quickly. So when they questioned me, I started questioning myself. I began having some concerns about it. I had already made up my mind this is what I was going to do and I did not want to deal with those questions or touch the feelings behind the questions. I knew if I started to open up to Diane about different people interfering in my mind, that she would sit there looking at me and I would explore feelings and issues that I did not want to look at.

SK: It sounds like you really were not feeling a lot of support about the engagement and didn't want to confront any issues that might have you question your decision.

BT: Yes, it's true.

SK: Did you ever get to address those with your therapist?

BT: No.

SK: Do you remember how you brought up ending therapy?

BT: I just told her that I was engaged and was going to be quitting work soon, and I was saving money for us to go away and pay for the wedding and stuff, and I just wanted to quit.

SK: What was the reaction?

BT: I think she asked me a couple of questions about feeling like I was ready to end. I was just real closed off at that point. I went in real happy-go-lucky and kind of had a wall up like there was no way she was going to get in. I wasn't going to let her talk me out of it. I went in to quit and there wouldn't have been much she could have said that would have made me open up at that point.

SK: Do you recall your therapist trying to make interpretations about your decision to end therapy at that point?

BT: No, at least it wasn't very direct. If it was, I ignored it— just turned it off. I don't remember feeling pressured or pushed by her. It was kind of like okay. I remember that she did make it clear that I could call her if I changed my mind next week. I do remember her saying I could come back at any time. Even though I had my wall up, I do remember feeling good about that.

SK: How many sessions did you have after your announcement of your decision to stop therapy?

BT: It was very short. I would say two at the most, but I went in ready to quit and there wasn't really much more I was ever going to talk about.

SK: It sounds like she respected your need to maintain the wall and live your own life.

BT: Yes. I think she just knew that at that point she didn't really have much hope of changing my mind about continuing therapy or looking at any of the feelings. She made it clear that if this is what I thought, that was okay, but please be sure to call her if I ever wanted to. That's how I remember it.

SK: Can you think back to the last two sessions? What happened?

BT: Specifically the last couple of sessions? No, I can't remember.

SK: Was there discussion about saying goodbye or any expression of missing each other initiated by her or you? Did she try to structure things in any way?

BT: Not that I remember. I might have been too closed off at the time to remember if she did since I'd already tuned her out. After I was gone, I wrote to her first, I'm pretty sure.

SK: After how long, do you think?

BT: Oh, probably after four months. I wrote to her and she wrote a real nice letter and mentioned some things in the letter that I'd worked through in therapy, that she hoped I'd remembered that I got to this point and not to backslide— some important things that at the time I read them felt great. I was very appreciative of her words of encouragement, about the progress I had made.

SK: It was like really doing some of the work you might have done if you had taken longer to end, and if you had not been so closed off.

BT: Yes! I never thought of it that way, but it was kind of a good ending when I was ready to hear.

SK: Do you remember what kinds of things you wrote?

BT: I just wrote her a letter telling her where I was at and what I was doing, how I felt in general. Nothing real earthshaking or like I wish I could come back and talk tomorrow or anything like that. It was just kind of a newsy, friendly type of letter.

SK: It sounds like she was never critical of your upcoming engagement or marriage, or even the way you decided to stop therapy.

BT: No, she wasn't ever critical at all about anything. She hardly ever really spoke [laughing]. Once in a while she asked a question or two, but she really was pretty quiet most of the time, and pretty much gave the questions right back to me. You know, like Why do you think that? What are you feeling? Why are you crying now? There were a couple of times when she made an interpretation and said in her opinion, but very seldom. She mostly made me question things within myself.

SK: Do you remember what you were feeling like in the last session as it was going on, or were you pretty numb?

BT: The only thing I can remember is I was just anxious to get out of my whole environment—out of work, out of therapy, away from anyone who would force me to look and question what I was doing.

SK: Were you aware that even though some people like your boss were putting pressure on you, that a part of you was scared about your plans and decisions?

BT: No, at first I was just angry. It was like they all had a lot of nerve. After a while I realized that's probably why I was so angry at everybody else, because they were mirroring what I was feeling and questioning myself. But at first I was mad at everybody because they were being so poopy.

SK: When you look back on it, was there anything your therapist could have done to make termination a better experience for you?

BT: I have never even felt, when I quit or later when I wrote her the letter, that there was anything she could have done or said that would have made me explore some of the issues more at that time.

SK: It actually sounds like it could have worked the opposite way, that you would have been angry at her.

BT: That's right. She would have been one more person on the list that I was mad at, probably, and then even therapy would have ended on a negative, angry note.

SK: It sounds like, right or wrong, you were making your own decision and could take responsibility yourself if it went well or not.

BT: Yes.

SK: Would you say she agreed or didn't agree with your decision to terminate therapy?

BT: I'd say she agreed. She seemed to accept it and wasn't reluctant. I think that she understood I needed just to get away, away from her, at that time.

SK: Her not being very intrusive seemed to be the correct response for you.

BT: Yes. I always thought she handled the situation well. I always liked her and I think that she helped me a lot during the time I was in there.

SK: Actually, that was going to be one of my next questions. Did you feel it's basically been a good experience for you?

BT: Yes, always. And if I wanted to go back in therapy, I would call her without hesitation. [Laughing.] Say, "Hey, remember me? Well, guess what?"

SK: It sounds like you would not have been so willing to enter treatment with her if she had been more intrusive, one of those people who were not supporting you.

BT: Right.

SK: So she actually never offered much structure. She didn't say, "Well, Barbara, I agree with you that it's really time you go, but the way I think we ought to do this is you should come in six or ten more times and talk about XYZ." She just followed your lead.

BT: I would say yes, she just followed my lead. I don't remember any discussion of we need to tie things up or end things or anything like that.

SK: It sounds like it just wasn't her style to structure things.

BT: She was very laid back, I'd say [laughing].

SK: Passive, neutral, reflecting your thoughts and feelings rather than pursuing her own agenda.

BT: Yes, that is exactly the way it was. I think she did just fine. I really don't think there was anything she could have said at the end that would have made me even think about doing anything differently. I'd already made up my mind to go on in and quit. Maybe five years later I would have thought about what she said. That's what she was trying to tell me that day!

SK: Do you think you'll ever go back into therapy again?

BT: I've thought about it a lot, in the last few years especially. Probably while I was married to Kevin I wouldn't because—this is going to sound really dumb to you—but only because he doesn't see it like I see it. He's never experienced it, for one thing. I don't think that he knows anybody except me that has. He thinks that you should be able to talk out and deal with whatever it is with a friend or spouse without going to somebody else and paying a lot of money, and they don't know anything anyway. That sort of an ignorant attitude. And it would just create a lot of conflict between us if I did. So that's one reason why I haven't. Unless I got really strong and said [laughing], "Listen!"

SK: If you were going to go back into therapy, would you do it in the same kind of way? Would you just go back to the same kind of person and set up the same open therapy model?

BT: Yeah, probably, because I liked the way Diane made me question things and figure them out for myself, rather than giving me advice, answers, or things to do. Friends who were in therapy talked about different methods that different therapists used. There were some that—and I know that it has a lot to do with the patient's interpretation of what the therapist was saying to them—people I knew were telling me things about the way their therapist dealt with them that were really wrong. Not outrageous, you know. Like telling them they needed to do this or needed to do that, even gave them ideas, like "you need to go on a vacation," and told them where to go. Really just took charge of their life. I'd rather make up my own mind and figure out my own things rather than someone telling me what I was feeling or why.

This patient began to feel that therapy could go on forever, and she acknowledged that it would be difficult to give up the therapeutic relationship at any point. She was afraid she might become a psychotherapy "addict" because of the unconditional positive regard, support, and empathy her therapist provided.

One of the important points in this example is that the clinician allowed the patient to seek the level of treatment with which she was comfortable. Ms. T. was struggling with dependency issues and perhaps was "fleeing" from a deep examination of her new relationship. Diane, the therapist, wisely did not confront her with leaving treatment and the possible connection between it and her engagement; Ms. T.'s self-disclosures show how correct the therapist's actions were. She admits that she was shut down emotionally and had one focus—to get married and leave treatment. She would not only have been unreceptive to confrontation about ending psychotherapy or explorations of her new relationship but she would have connected the therapist and the therapy to all the unsupportive people in her life. The clinician aptly perceived that the client "could not be talked out of ending therapy," and resisted the temptation to make manipulative interpretations. By letting the patient go, the therapist truly enabled her to grow and gain independence. Ms. T. assuredly made mistakes, but this is the only way to become more autonomous.

A Negative Termination

The following interview with Brian A. illustrates almost every element of a negative termination experience. The therapist's countertransference issues were so blatant that even the client asked her if something going on in her extratherapy life was affecting his treatment.

SK: Can you tell me before we talk about the ending of therapy what brought you in for therapy? Why you went for help?

BA: I began therapy because of a relationship falling apart. I discovered that my wife was having an affair. In the course of those early traumatic days, we had some very bad fights and I had some violent feelings. Being that far out of control frightened me badly. I needed some immediate help, which worked. Then after the immediate crisis was sort of under control, at least to the point where I could deal with it somewhat, I still continued. The total time was about one and three-quarters years. We were digging into the root causes of my problems, not just talking about the marriage.

SK: So first you dealt with the immediate crisis, then you continued in treatment to focus on the longer term issues.

BA: Yes. It turns out that a lot of the longer term issues had quite a bit to do with the relationship problems, too. And the fact that the root of my problems was being sort of benignly psychologically neglected by my mother. I don't think she ever meant to. I don't think she ever thought she did. But she did some things that messed me up pretty good. I sort of had this underlying resentment of women. I had a tendency, I think, to subconsciously pick women similar to my mother's personality. And then when they did begin to act like her, I would become the rebellious kid. That's basically what we worked on.

SK: Can you tell me about the ending of your therapy?

BA: Yes. We got to the ending part and, well, what I felt was we weren't really winding down. We weren't going anywhere for several sessions.

SK: Do you remember talking about that?

BA: I was feeling that I was stuck, that maybe we were both stuck. It wasn't that I didn't think there were other things to work on. There probably is always more to work on. I felt we were stuck there. And I had been told several times by the therapist, well, we're just about done. That had gone on six months before. I said, look, are we just about finished with this?

SK: Do you think during that six-month period you had been making clear noises about ending therapy?

BA: I had said several times that I was thinking about ending for the last six months, yes. The overriding practical reasons were both financial and emotional. I've thought about this deeply—the financial part was real, not an excuse. It got to the point where it was a real financial burden to pay for therapy. I was scared about paying regular bills. And I felt like I had made a lot of progress. It wasn't that I felt deep down there wasn't anything to work on. I felt there were things that we could probably work on forever.

SK: It sounds like you felt in a sense that there are always more issues and conflicts to work out, but at that point there was nothing really pressing. You had done a fair amount of good work and coupled with the financial burden, you wanted to stop.

BA: Right.

SK: You were feeling—let me know if I'm putting words in your mouth—that you might have continued if finances were better, but on the other hand, maybe not. I mean, you were doing pretty well.

BA: No, no, you're not putting words in my mouth. If finances were not a problem, I might have continued. Probably the money was the straw, so to speak. I was not in pain anymore. And I knew that I could function pretty well. Not that there weren't other things to work on and other problems, because there were.

SK: So you would bring it up and the therapist would say, well, we're getting there?

BA: Yeah, and when I would bring up the money problems as well, she would only say, "If you want to do this, you'll find a way." And then I started feeling very pressured for the money. And that sort of accelerated the process in my head of saying, look, I've just got to do something. And it was not what I would call an amicable, really amicable parting, either.

SK: In the six-month period you would bring it up, she would kind of say if you really wanted to continue, you'll find a way. You would passively agree, but you were feeling hurt and increasingly angry.

BA: I felt horrible about it—misunderstood. Inside, yes, I was going. I was thinking about going and it wasn't that we didn't work on things and accomplish things during that time. We did.

SK: But it was like it was all played to the background of feeling misunderstood and getting ready to leave.

BA: Yeah, I was beginning to feel really pressured. What I do want to point out as far as the therapy is concerned, the therapist was wonderful and did extremely good work. We did extremely good work together.

SK: It was a good experience.

BA: Oh, yes, overall a good experience. The ending part was, I think, more of an irritation to the therapist.

SK: Did it not leave you with some negative feelings as well?

BA: Yes it did.

SK: It's like you had this really good experience and then, at the end, it changed.

BA: Yes, but it did not destroy all my good feelings about the therapy.

SK: How did the actual ending come about? Do you remember?

BA: Well, we had this arrangement, because of my job being an actor, that cancellations would happen and could happen at the last minute because I'm simply not given a lot of notice many times when I have to be somewhere for an audition.

SK: So your therapist and you agreed upon that?

BA: Yeah, and that got to be a real thorn in the therapist's side later on.

SK: But it wasn't, prior to the ending?

BA: No. Well, I'm leading up to that. The actual ending came about when I had one of these cancellations. And she got quite angry.

SK: Had there been other times?

BA: Oh, yeah, yeah.

SK: Was she angry then?

BA: Well, I definitely sensed some irritation at times. And then right at the end I don't know whether it had anything to do with it anyway. I called her on the phone and told her I had an audition the next day. It was early evening. And she got quite angry about it. And I said, look, the fact that I can pay for this at all depends on what I do, you know. If I don't do this, then we have nothing to talk about because it is how I make a living.

SK: And she knew this?

BA: Yes, she apologized. I don't know if she was having a bad time at home on her own or what. But she apologized for that, for getting angry, or as she said, the confrontation. She was pissed. I can tell when somebody is pissed, and she was pissed. I said, "All of this was discussed at the beginning of therapy. This is not new. We both agreed to make the best of the situation at the start. But the fact that this is irritating you this much at this point is unfortunate, but it isn't something you didn't know."

I know where she's coming from, she's in business. It chopped part of her day out that she could have used to earn a living. I never was under any illusions that she was doing this out of her Mother Theresa syndrome. She's in business and I understand that.

And then I just called her and said, "That's it." And she was really upset and wanted to be paid for the session that I cancelled. Which I did not do. And I didn't do it because I couldn't scrape up the money. I could have. I did it because of the prior agreement that we had had about it. If the agreement had been different, then I would have paid. For me it became a matter of principle at that point. I've thought since from time to time of just sending her the money for it, but never have. Sometime I feel like maybe I ought to do that.

SK: Well, let me check this out with you. Is this what you're saying happened? It sounds like you were grappling with leaving for a long time. Subtly, your therapist encouraged you not to stop, saying there is still more to work on but we are almost there. So you continued, but it was never the same because in a sense you really wanted to leave months earlier.

BA: Yes.

SK: It's like this incident about the so-called missed or cancelled appointment was a way for both of you to act out your feelings about the process and a way for you to finally terminate. It sounds like you would have ended anyway, but this

was an opportunity. Your therapist was not responding well
to your earlier ending noises, your need to terminate.

BA: It was the excuse and opportunity.

SK: To get out.

BA: To get out, and I used it.

SK: It seems that not throughout the course of therapy,
because you really felt that she was a good therapist, but during the ending process it sounds like she was acting very
much like your mom. Not being very responsive to your
needs.

BA: Exactly! It was pretty overt, actually. I felt it was an
overreaction and my honest feeling was that something happened to her life unrelated to me and it spilled out on me.
Because even though I knew that it was always a source of
irritation, when these rare cancellations occurred, she was
never so overtly angry. I wouldn't like it either. I understand
that. But it is essential for me to have that flexibility to make
a living.

SK: It wasn't optimal for either one of you. But it was what
you both agreed to. So a big part of what you were feeling is
kind of misunderstood. I mean, there was an agreement made.

BA: Yes, I felt that somebody had changed the rules on me.
And I was saying, whoa!, if that's the way it's going to be
from now on, this is a good time to end it.

SK: She might have had some things going on in her life,
but also she might have been having a difficult time letting
you go. She was not handling the ending very well.

BA: Yeah. Well, as a matter of fact, the first therapy I had—
the group—was ended by the therapist. He said, "That's it,
you don't need anymore of this. It's enough." That was
the only time that's ever happened, which I always really
respected him for. Saying, "Look, we really don't have any
more to work on."

SK: Do you have any thoughts or opinions about the whole ending process that I haven't asked you about?

BA: Only that I felt bad about it. I had this feeling like, gee whiz, I didn't want it to end in this angry way with the therapist demanding money. And I felt that in a way I had been kind of betrayed. When all of a sudden it became very mercenary. That didn't make me angry so much as it hurt me.

SK: And that's what kind of reminded me of your mother.

BA: Yeah. Anytime that I needed to cancel, I didn't fake a cancellation. They were all real. That's why I felt kind of bad about the last one. If I had done this just to avoid therapy, that would be one thing, but I didn't.

SK: In that six-week period, do you remember what you were uncomfortable, about? What was happening?

BA: The underlying thing always was the fact that I was running out of money. I wasn't running out, but it was getting to the point where I was extremely worried.

SK: You were pretty preoccupied with worrying about money. Your worrying about it was overshadowing what was going on in the sessions?

BA: It's hard to know. I can't really decide because accomplishments were made during that period of time, but not in the last month. I don't think we accomplished much.

SK: Brian, if you could turn back the clock and do some things differently, and especially have your therapist do some things differently, what kind of ending would you liked to have seen? How would you have liked to end?

BA: It would have been more optimal for me if she would have understood what I was telling her. That I was having extreme cash-flow problems at the time and that I thought we were stuck and that I did not have any problem with reestablishing therapy under more favorable conditions financially. And to have her understand that.

SK: It sounds like that's what you felt—she didn't understand. Did she ever interpret your leaving as a resistance or avoidance of issues?

BA: I think so. I mean, I don't think she ever really came right out and said that, but she certainly implied it. "If you just try harder, you can find the money," she would say. If I really wanted to continue. "And if you really wanted to, you'd even borrow the money." You know that kind of feeling. And I was saying, wow. I was deeply in hock to my dentist for all sorts of work, too. We're talking thousands of dollars.

SK: That's just what you're saying, that your bills and your financial straits were real—they weren't a resistance or an avoidance.

BA: Right!

SK: And that's what she couldn't comprehend in some way.

BA: Either couldn't or wouldn't.

SK: So you would have had things go differently in your ideal. She would have understood.

BA: Yeah. "I understand that you can't do this now, but I think maybe in the future we might start again under more favorable conditions to you. And when you feel that's in your best interest, give me a call and we'll do it." That's the kind of response that would have felt great.

SK: Leaving the door open.

BA: Yes, and leave the door open. In effect, she slammed it. But that wouldn't preclude using her again. I wouldn't automatically. Just because she responded that way didn't diminish my feeling that she was a good therapist.

SK: In your ideal, with her probably understanding much earlier—six weeks, two months earlier—how many sessions would you have taken to kind of say goodbye or end or wrap things up? Do you have any idea about that? What would you have been comfortable with?

BA: I would imagine three, four, about that. That would have been comfortable. But it was just like any time I would say, "Look, I'm sorry but I just can't," she was giving me no assistance to help sort of wrap things up. As I mentioned to her, too, I said, "Look, I don't think there's anything to work on that it isn't something we couldn't pick up and work on in the future. You know, we've made enough progress, you've helped me enough that I can function pretty well without a great deal of problems. And so, for the time being I'd like to do that. But I never got an understanding response. I hoped that I would, but I just didn't. I just remembered something about that final phone call, or that final cancellation. She did angrily remind me that this was her business, that she depended on it for her income. Which I said I understood, but I reminded her she also understood the conditions of the therapy when we began. And then she did call back and apologize—not really apologize, she said, "I guess I was rather confrontational." I said, "Well, you sounded very angry."

SK: Pissed off [laughing].

BA: Right [laughing]. I used those words. I did say, "You're angry. And I don't know whether you're angry at me or somebody else, but you're angry." And that was enough for me at that point to say, "Okay, that's it. Well, that's a real good idea, yes."

  If I were to go back to somebody new for psychotherapy, one of the first questions I would ask is about how they like to end therapy. I would want to know that. "How do you feel about this? Do *you* have a difficult time letting people out of therapy? Do you see a point when they can function okay and does it bother you if they decide to end and you don't agree? Are we going to have a big scene when I end or what?" Because having had a big scene, it was real uncomfortable and it made me feel kind of bad.

  This treatment unfolds in a manner common in open-ended psychotherapy. The patient presents in a crisis state with specific issues to work on. Within months, he is doing extremely well. The therapist, not inappropriately, encourages the patient to explore longer-term underlying reasons for his current life problems. The patient, very representative of clients seen in out-patient, open-ended treatment, has difficulties of a narcissistic nature. They proceed together on this course of self-discovery and enter the "timeless zone," with its boundlessness and goallessness.

This sets the tone for the acting out that follows. The client continues to improve and then decides to end, based on a cost/benefit analysis. The therapist does everything in her power to avoid issues of termination and, in effect, blames the patient for wanting to stop treatment. "If you really wanted to continue, you would find a way." "You are not quite ready yet." Clearly he is; it is the therapist who is not ready to let go. Not understanding the patient's needs and feelings in an empathic manner serves to restimulate injuries to the self that the client sustained in childhood. At some level, the patient feels this as familiar and bad treatment that he deserves. As he protected his mother, he is protecting the therapist. Both therapist and client act out the ending since the therapist is not prepared to offer the client the type of assistance he needs to end in a healthy, self-enhancing way.

Clearly, it was the therapist's countertransference issues that sabotaged the ending of B. A.'s treatment. In contrast, the clinician in the first case epitomizes the philosophy and spirit that should guide the termination process, especially when a client wishes to end and the therapist believes the client is in error or is resisting working through issues. The balance tipped for the second therapist when she put her needs above the psychological and economic needs of the client.

The Issue of Fees

Sometimes a disagreement about fees can be the catalyst to end a treatment that is stuck or ready to finish, although this subject may not be overtly discussed by either therapist or client. Even if the economic issue is not the best reason to terminate, perhaps it is better to have such a catalyst rather than continue treatment endlessly with increasingly diminishing returns.

At other times, however, the classical analytic rigidity about the problem of fees may have a deleterious effect on a treatment that is not winding down naturally. I was taught in supervision and graduate training classes that clients—without exception—should be charged for missed or failed sessions, no matter what the reason. Although I tried to maintain this inflexible policy in my practice, I soon learned that such dogmatic adherence to theory (incidentally, unsupported by research) was not helpful to my patients. I do charge someone who takes advantage of my leniency by missing appointments for careless reasons, even if the client is angry or threatens to terminate; I am more concerned about the symbolic meaning to the treatment than the actual money. But my research indicates that an intractable policy about fees is experienced by patients, especially certain types of clients, as a deep wound, a narcissistic injury.

This experience was told to me during an interview with a thirty-five-year-old woman who had been in psychoanalytic psychotherapy for almost two years. She was a high-functioning but characterologically troubled person exhibiting low self-esteem, depression, and an inability to assert herself. One day, a few hours before a treatment session, she received a message that her mother was being rushed to an emergency room. She phoned her therapist, found he was out, left a message with his office, and proceeded to attend to her dying mother. The therapist charged her for the session, stating at their next appointment, "I am sorry about your mother, but I could not fill the time slot at such late notice." This contributed a trauma to the patient's self from which she never recovered. She terminated her sessions after approximately six weeks. The practitioner clung to theoretical prescriptions blindly and too rigidly; a more empathic consideration might have led him to understand how his demand for payment would affect the patient under those circumstances.

In another example, a twenty-seven-year-old man, who had been in psychodynamic treatment for more than four years, missed a session when a massive downpour and flood hit his community. Phone lines were out, travel was impossible, and he was obliged to try to save his home and his valuables. In spite of all this, the therapist charged him for the missed session. This patient experienced the charge as a slap in the face. He left treatment with a great deal of appropriate anger at the therapist and bitter feelings about psychotherapy in general.

In a similar case but with a very different outcome, a forty-four-year-old man, who had been in therapy for five years because of a borderline personality disorder, had car problems on the way to a session. He was forced to stop at a service station, and quite upset, called the therapist to ask if he could come in later. The therapist was able to accommodate the request. On the way to the second session three hours later, the unlucky client had a flat tire and was unable to make the appointment. At the next scheduled session, the therapist said he would not charge the patient for the missed appointments because circumstances had been beyond his control and he did not want to be punitive. Tears welled up in the client's eyes; his expression as well as his words told the deep meaning this had for him. By empathically responding in deed and words, the therapist had offered a corrective emotional experience. His response had profound significance for the client, who had experienced in early childhood and throughout his adult life only criticism and harshness from other men.

Self-injuries can be inflicted by practitioners over many issues, but especially the issue of fees. This is a subject that demands particular sensitivity. Therapists need to take great care to consider the client's point of view in order to avoid a therapeutic intervention that the client may construe as unreasonable or even cruel, and that may actually injure a client's fragile self structure.

7

Final Sessions: Differing Scenarios

It was interesting to note that the data from my formal studies reveal a lighter emphasis on loss or separation in final sessions than on other categories—quite a bit less than might be expected from the theoretical literature. In a minority of cases, there was no direct focus on termination. (Several interpretations of this and other findings will be discussed below.) In very few cases, clients simply failed to show up for the last appointment.

Generally, the characteristics of the last session include some treatment review and focus on the therapist/client relationship. Therapist F. L. covers most of the primary elements of treatment review when he describes a last session with one of his patients: "We reviewed the process of treatment, the issues she came in with and how they had been addressed, evoking from her a summary of treatment and what she got out of it and how she saw herself using it after termination."

Some practitioners refer to the issue of loss in the last hours. Therapist A. C. reports: "I let people know that they might reexperience some feelings about losses and that we would explore them together." Therapist N. E. says that she and her patients talk about the difficulty of saying goodbye.

Therapist O. T. describes a "more open discussion of what we felt about each other." She reports: "In the last session I move away from a professional to a more equalized sharing, peer quality, in the relationship. I talk more directly about my feelings toward the client."

I also observed from my research a low incidence of regression in the termination phase and, specifically, in the final therapeutic hour. This appears to be in opposition to the psychodynamic and classical analytic axiom that regression and possibly a temporary return of symptoms, is to be expected as the ending nears. The low occurrence of regression may reflect the high percentage of client-initiated terminations, implying that clients may fare better if the treatment ending is initiated by them. This is certainly in keeping with the humanistic tenet that outside and inside the therapeutic setting people need to be proactive and do best when they move to their own inner rhythm.

The reporting of loss and separation seems to be less than the clinical literature and folklore might suggest. One reason may be that both practitioners and patients have trouble dealing with the painful issue of loss. Not discussing the impending separation may reflect an avoidance or denial of its impact. Perhaps in a longer-term treatment, this issue would be worked through before the final sessions. Or possibly the respondents felt that loss and separation is such an integral part of termination that everyone understands that it just occurs.

Therapist H. W. expresses an uncommon and interesting perspective: "I think ending, and specifically the last session, is not such a big deal as I thought it was. I used to make termination a larger issue than it really is. Now I encourage people to look at their program and if they need to come back and work on an issue, they can." Perhaps this view is related to therapist H. W.'s shift from a psychodynamic orientation to a more problem-solving behavioral approach to treatment. This quote could also characterize a practitioner who has developed a defensive posture to protect himself from potentially painful emotions.

Termination with No Final Session

Among the most difficult situations for therapists are those where there are no final sessions, no closure to the therapeutic relationship: abrupt terminations and vanishing clients. Perhaps the need for closure is a primary reason for some therapists too aggressively pursuing patients who suddenly disappear.

Abrupt Terminations. Occasionally a client may end the therapeutic work on short notice or no notice at all. When this happens to me, I feel it as an injury to my self. I would like to believe that I am too personally secure to have such feelings but, like most people, I am susceptible to being hurt when someone close to me leaves suddenly. However, I am also comfortable with my vulnerability and fragility because these emotions mean I am open to my client. The humanist within me is taken aback when someone who has shared his or her secret self does not attend the final session or vanishes without a verbal announcement. The scientist within me seeks explanations for this complex process and strongly desires to learn so that I can be a better clinician and teacher.

There are no clear guidelines to follow when faced with these situations. Each case must be conducted on an individual basis, with treatment theory acting as a backdrop. A certain type of nondirectiveness is espoused by classical psychodynamic theory, client-centered theory, and other analytic schools such as the model propagated by Kohut. Practically speaking, however, no matter what the theory, it is quite difficult to maintain a balanced perspective when it comes to clients who suddenly end treatment.

For example, a woman I had seen in open-ended treatment suddenly ended her therapy. I believe that she was actually doing too well, and this frightened her. Ms. Ruth K. was closer than she had ever been to ending her long-standing, abusive marriage, but she was afraid of functioning as an autonomous and free person. At the same time, she was very troubled by her dependency on me. She accused me of pressuring her to leave her husband, and this projection rapidly took on a psychotic transference character. By eliminating me she was, I believe, ridding herself of conflict that she feared would fragment her vulnerable self structure.

Although most of her extreme feelings were a projection and form of transference, there was a core of truth to her perception that I did not support her marriage and encouraged her to move toward relationships that would provide sustenance and affirmation. As her self-esteem and sense of identity grew stronger, it became obvious to both of us that her marital relationship was a destructive influence. If I made an error, it was that I was not empathically connected to how very fearful Ms. K. felt about ending such a long-standing relationship. No matter how bad it was, she obviously still needed it at some level. It is certainly plausible that in my eagerness to encourage her to grow and change, I did not attend enough to the part of her that valued her husband and depended on him.

Our last meeting was not intended to be our final session. Ms. K. entered my office in a distant and quietly angry mood. I reflected to her what I perceived with no interpretation, only that she appeared aloof and angry. She agreed and said I just did not seem to understand her. She was wondering if I could still help her since I was against her husband and her marriage. In some ways I felt I had lost her already or vice versa. I had tried in the preceding weeks to convince her of my neutrality and point out that she was the one living in the situation, that whether she remained in the marriage or left it would have little bearing on my life personally. I had said that nothing would make me happier than helping her work out the marital conflicts if she wanted to and if it was possible.

In what became the final hour, Ms. K. expressed strong criticism of me and my approach, but she clearly did not want me to respond. She had decided to end treatment and used numerous defense mechanisms to support her departure, although she alluded a few times to there being some room for "us" to work things out. She ended the session with a distant, forced politeness, almost as she had behaved eighteen months before when she began treatment. The warmth, close-ness, and other positive aspects of the relationship were not present at all. Three days before her next scheduled visit, she left a message that she no longer needed my services because she could not afford them anymore. Nothing had changed monetarily. Although I had known that she probably would terminate treatment, I was somewhat shocked and hurt, not only because of her abruptness but also her manner in carry-ing it out. Intellectually I understood the dynamics, but I felt depreciated.

When such a termination takes place, how should the practitioner respond? What behavior of mine would have been beneficial for Ms. K.? If I phoned her, I would not be respecting her desire to avoid discussion and would com-pound what she perceived as my intrusiveness. If I were to receive the message and do nothing, I would be respecting her personal autonomy. However, she might interpret this no-contact, no-response attitude as my not caring about her and perhaps reinforcing her feeling that I was disappointed in her because she did not end her destructive relationship.

After thinking the issue through, I decided a balanced response might be to write a brief note. My intention was to acknowledge the phone call, to convey that I understood through an empathic response and connected mild interpre-tation, and to remind her that even in her anger and fear I still cared and my door would remain open to her. In my note, I gently confronted her with my understanding of the reason for her flight. If I were able to turn back time, I would now write the letter without an interpretation or confronta-tion. Immediately upon receiving it, she called and left a mes-sage saying, "Tell Dr. Kramer I do not want any more therapy or letters from him."

It is impossible to predict whether no response from me, or the note minus interpretation or confrontation, would have produced a different outcome. Further experience has reinforced for me what Kohut said about most confrontations in psychotherapy: that they are usually more for the clini-cian's benefit than the client's.

Vanishing Patients. Even less satisfactory than a client's abrupt decision to leave therapy is the sudden disappearance, without warning, of someone you have been seeing regularly. Disappearing clients give no observable cues that they intend to end psychotherapy, or even that they are upset about something. At times I have been able to identify clients who are predisposed to leave treatment in such a manner. Sometimes I have been able to help clients not vanish by sharing these thoughts—actually predicting that they will disappear. This, of course, does not always work. A successful example of this paradoxical technique involved Wayne N., who presented with severe characterological difficulties and reported numerous therapeutic contacts that never lasted more than six months. He had also been involved in a long series of brief and superficial interpersonal relationships, always ending with his disappearance. I predicted that he would vanish from treatment in about six months. This paradoxical technique helped him to change his long-standing pattern: He successfully ended treatment after eighteen months with the ability to form more lasting relationships.

Patients who are most predisposed to disappear without cues tend to be individuals who flee from intimacy and dependency and who have a history of brief, superficial relationships that end abruptly. They come to treatment with severe psychopathologies, such as borderline or severe narcissistic personalities, or ambulatory psychoses. These extremely vulnerable clients are less able than others to verbalize the self injuries that normally occur during the therapeutic process or that are brought on by the therapist's countertransference issues. Such a patient is likely to be someone who has been traumatized repeatedly at an early age and whose life has been devoid of nurturing, life-sustaining self-objects.

An example of this is Ms. Eileen H., a twenty-year-old victim of incest, who was in psychotherapy for just over a year with Dr. Charles S. The therapist discussed the issue of Ms. H. seeing a female practitioner, but the patient chose to work with him. She felt that she trusted him as much as she could trust anyone. The treatment appeared to be going well, so when she vanished, Dr. S. was unprepared. In an interview, he stated:

> The termination took me totally by surprise. She was making progress with her self-esteem, direction in life, and she even was making headway with her boyfriend. Of course, the theme of the incest was dealt with as it related to all aspects of her self and life. One day she just didn't show up for an appointment. I was concerned, of course, and called. I believe she had her number changed or disconnected with no forwarding number. I wrote her, with no response. She had an outstanding balance, so I also sent a statement. Again, no response.
>
> Finally, I tracked her down at work. I will always regret this conversation. It was very clear she did not want to talk—she sounded scared. In my anxiety to have her try to hear me, I was probably too aggressive, not sensitive enough, and inadvertently reinforced her worst fears and feelings. I remember saying things like, "What happened? How can you just stop? I'm not your father."

Dr. S. was upset with himself for not sensing something was wrong; he was shocked, and he felt abandoned at some level. Because of this combination of feelings, he acted out some emotions that should have been dealt with in an extra-treatment context. It is not difficult to identify with Dr. S.'s feelings. His retrospective analysis was that the patient had an acute psychotic transference. The therapist had become the abusive, intrusive father, and she was running for her physical and psychological life.

What should Dr. S. have done differently, if anything? In regard to this termination, perhaps doing less would have been best. After not getting a response to his letters and phone messages, he probably should not have pursued the patient. Her lack of response was a clear statement that she needed to be left alone, at least by her therapist, at that point in time. It was the practitioner who felt cheated. His need for closure and understanding of what happened are clearly normal and understandable. As therapists, however, we do not have the luxury of acting on our own needs in treatment situations. Dr. S.'s termination error was attempting to get closure at his patient's expense.

In an illustration from my own practice, a twenty-seven-year-old woman entered psychotherapy with me because of an eating disorder and other personality issues. The treatment proceeded very well: She stopped her bulimic behavior and was learning to deal with her underlying anger in productive and healthy ways.

Then we began to focus on her relationships with men. She had not been able to sustain a relationship for more than a month before the fear of intimacy and dependency became so overwhelming that she would sabotage the relationship. During this time, she met a man with whom she became intensely involved. A few weeks later, she failed to show up for a regular appointment. I phoned and left two messages, with no response. Finally, I wrote her a letter that told her my door was open if she wanted to either wrap up treatment or continue it. Again, no response came. As I am prone to do in such ambiguous endings, I spent a lot of time examining the possible transference and countertransference issues. Had I said or done something that caused the patient to experience a narcissistic injury?

Typically, I focused more on the unfinished treatment than I did on the remarkable changes she had made in a short time. Experience has taught me that this is a problem for many practitioners and that it seems connected to the need to strive for perfect therapeutic outcomes. It is a question of whether the cup is half full or half empty.

However, to my surprise, this client phoned three years later and asked to return for further treatment. She explained that she had vanished because she did not want to work any more on her relationships with men. Instead, she rushed into a marriage to avoid the issue. It was no surprise that now she was having marital troubles and was ready to explore further her relationship problems. I must admit it was gratifying when she thanked me profusely for all that I had helped her accomplish earlier. She was reminding me that when she left therapy on her own terms, her cup was more than half full.

Transcription of a Final Session

Following is an annotated transcription of an actual final session between a client, Roger, and his therapist, Judith. Roger had been in therapy with Judith for approximately three years. His presenting problems were depression and low self-esteem. Progress had been gradual but continual, and termination was initiated by the client, with the therapist agreeing and supporting him in his decision.

Roger: There's been a great deal of moving around at work. When corporations start transferring and moving people around—what do you do with people on their way out? It's only in the last few years that corporations have given any consideration to helping someone who is no longer employed by them to find other employment, or where corporations moving from Chicago to the Sun Belt help an employee who can't move there. In the olden days, they just moved and said so long and see you later.

He is speaking in metaphors about ending.

Judith: Well, that's interesting that your field is starting to pay attention . . .

Roger: Hopefully, it's corporations are becoming more aware of employing *people* rather than employing bookkeepers and engineers. I don't think they've really gone that far, but they are a little more open.

Judith: Some people get *terminated* and are told . . .

Roger: Terminated is a good word, too.

Judith: . . . an hour before to pack your stuff and get out of here.

Roger: In many ways that's a very effective way of ending because if you say, "Hey, Joe, it's been great, you've been a wonderful employee and you've got two weeks," you are better off saying, "You're finished today, I'm going to give you two week's pay and your vacation and whatever else, and you might as well leave today," because the two weeks becomes not only nonproductive but tends to become destructive because the person is trapped at this desk doing nothing. There is nothing to plan for.

Are they talking about personal styles of wanting to end?

Judith: Still, it seems kind of inhumane.

Roger: Well, it's quick, and people don't like periods of transition.

Judith: Some of us do, right?

Roger: Some of us need it more than others.

Therapist brings him to the business of the final session.

Judith: In fact, I'm trying to think of what I said when you didn't

come to that last appointment. I
think I said you were feeling pretty
good and things were going okay
and you didn't really need to come,
but I asked you to come once more
so we could kind of wrap it up.

Roger: I thought a great deal about
that missed appointment. Because
that's not my normal way of doing
things. A long time ago I went to a
psychiatrist and I complained to
him that I had gone out with some
people and there was a long row,
and I ended up sitting at the end.
He said, "Well, hey, you put yourself at the end. They didn't put you
at the end, you just put yourself
there and created a situation for
yourself." So I thought to myself,
by missing that appointment what
was I really saying? I never write
sessions down. I've got them right
here [points to head], every one of
them.

Client continues to
intellectualize, thus
avoiding saying
goodbye.

Judith: I didn't know that's how
you did it. I know that it was
highly unusual for that to happen.

Roger: Well, I've never had to
write one down. You can change
the dates and times, and I always
remember. I must have been block-
ing the appointment, or whatever.
Because the week before, I said to
myself, I've got to call Judith
because I can't make this, I can't
remember the reason, and it kept

It is important for
him to show his
intelligence and
maintain control.

just getting pushed out of my mind.
I'd forget about it, then I'd remember it. Then it got to the point,
even that day, I said I've got to call,
and it got pushed out of my head.

Judith: Could you have been angry
with me?

Roger: I don't know. In asking the
question, you generate the thought.
I don't know if it was anger. I
doubt it was anger because I have a
lot of affection for you and a lot of
respect for you.

Judith: That doesn't mean you
can't be angry with me.

Roger: No, I think it was almost
the thought that I was saying goodbye, that you don't want to say
goodbye to somebody. Well, as I tell
you about it, I can feel emotions
coming up that I didn't feel before I
got here—before we discussed it.
But maybe the best way to explain
it is when someone has been as
great a help to me as you have, and
someone has been patient and kind
and all the things I feel, that you
really don't want to say goodbye,
but in a way you are. You're saying
you've done your job and you've
done it well, but maybe I wanted to
find an excuse to come back. I
think that's what comes to mind
about missing that last appointment—not wanting to face the fact.

At this point, the
client is more in
touch with his
feelings.

He is right on
target.

Judith: I know what you mean about those feelings. It is also difficult for me to say goodbye to you. I will think of you fondly and wonder how you are doing.

Good job of self-disclosing and affirming his feelings.

Roger: There was a period in the last several months where the lights just went on and everything just started falling together. There have been times since we talked last that I've been down and really felt depressed, and all of the other things. But I was able to work my way out of it—that's the whole key. And it's not that I don't need somebody who is bright and perceptive to talk to me. I'm never going to talk to anybody bright and perceptive again. [She laughs.] But there isn't that desperate need that was there where I didn't know, I just didn't have any answers. I could not solve my problems.

Problems continue but he has tools to deal with them. He feels proud.

I'm satisfied with the solutions that I've come up with to solve my problems. They may not be perfect or the best or the greatest, but they seem to be satisfactory for where I am. And there's a feeling of either peace or contentment, just satisfaction, that is there. Now, we were talking about that missed appointment. Now, tonight I feel differently. It's sort of a happy occasion for both you and for me. It's a sense of accomplishment; it's what we're here for and what we're doing.

Roger expresses the fact that he has sought out the level of treatment which he, not the therapist, wishes.

I went out to dinner with
Sue, Bob, the kids and my mother. I
just happened to be in town and
they just happened to be going out
to dinner because Jennifer is going
away to college tomorrow.

Judith: You mean tonight, earlier?

Roger: Yeah, I just ran from the restaurant to here.

Judith: My goodness!

Roger: I don't know how anybody
else felt, but I felt terrific.

Judith: That's great.

Roger: Usually when I'm with Bob
or his father, I always feel like I
should get a grip on the chair
because I'm going to be attacked at
any moment and feel inadequate in
some way. And I didn't at all.

Judith: Was Henry there, too?

Roger: Oh, he was there, too, and
his wife. It was a very pleasant evening. He got wine spilled on him
and he still felt good. Maybe he
started drinking before he got to the
restaurant. Everybody had a good
time and the food was excellent. It
was a very pleasant, nice time.
I had gone over to see Sue
before dinner. We had a nice conversation about a lot of things we
hadn't talked over in a long time. I
think what made me think about

ending was the last time I was here,
sort of like this time, I spent the
whole hour talking about how great
I felt. That's not bad, because I
spent a lot of time talking about
how lousy I felt. There's no real
productive point after a certain time
of coming back and just telling you
how great I feel. If I feel good, well
then, okay, let's end the sessions.

This shows his
gradual turnabout.

Judith: I think the description that
you mentioned earlier is kind of a
real marker of when it's time. Early
on, when a person feels desperate,
there is no question about continuing. When it starts to feel like "I
feel good and there isn't that much
to talk about," it is time to be
thinking about ending.

Therapist reiterates
the cost/benefit
analysis.

Roger: I think things started to
change with the session where the
revelation of why I was here, why I
had come all these times, to have
you help solve my problems to finding out that you were helping me
solve my *own* problems, coming up
with my *own* answers. I've probably
told any number of people who are
considering therapy or who are in
therapy that that was the revelation
for me. Maybe it will be a revelation for them. For me that was
important. It was certainly a boost
for my own self-esteem to realize
that I could solve my own problems
to my satisfaction.

Illustrates the
axiom, "If I catch
you a fish, you eat
for a day. But if I
teach you to fish,
you eat for a
lifetime."

Judith: It feels great to know you are important and can find your own solutions.

Roger: Well, I'll tell you how much it counted. Just last week I got into another discussion with my boss about a number of different things. I was at my absolute best. I'm really a terrible ham. [She laughs.] I can act almost any part and I really try to make him feel as bad as possible. I succeeded because I know that when he gets nervous, he starts to get cotton in his mouth and I could see him almost gasping for air. So I know I had him on the ropes and I just kept punching away.

Judith: I'm laughing because I'm well aware of what a role reversal from the times when he really had you on the ropes.

They are proud of their work together and interact warmly and with spontaneity.

Roger: That's not all over, because I haven't gone through a total change. I'm still the same person with some changes. But I'm better aware of who I am and what I have and what I can do. I put an article in his mailbox—I still couldn't hand it to him. It was in my soccer coach's manual and had to do with building and not destroying, and letting kids play their own game without having to comment every step of the way. I've got it in my briefcase. I thought you might enjoy reading it; I'll put it in the mail to

It is true he has not reformed his personality or built a new character structure. He has changed, however, and is leaving treatment because he has met his own termination criteria.

you. Every time I read it, I've gotten sort of emotional because it's so true. I hope he understands what the article says about letting people do things their own way and not having to be after them all the time.

    That's one of the things that I appreciated about our sessions. I can think of a lot of dumb statements that I made, and you could have said, "Don't think that way, think this way," but you let me work things out for myself. I tried things and if they didn't work, then I tried something else. I found the answer without being pushed toward an answer. That was important to me. Because I think a lot of my life has been spent having people push me toward the answers.

Judith: I know. I don't believe in doing that. I really think that what you're talking about is extremely important and something I feel strongly about, and feel it is much more worthwhile for people to figure out their own solutions if I can help them do the looking. I appreciate that you were aware of that.

Roger: Oh, yeah, very important, very important.

Judith: The other side of it, though, Roger, is that you hung in there and worked and struggled. I couldn't supply that.

His comments about children growing relate metaphorically to how he has changed and grown in the therapeutic setting.

What he experienced in therapy.

He speaks of the whole treatment process as well as the termination phase.

She is nonjudgmental, noncritical, nondirective— facilitating, not trying to fix or mold him.

She does a good job of accepting some affirmation, but refocuses on the client's will and proactive strivings.

Roger: What I notice the most is feeling better about myself. There is still a small corner that could be better. But in some way it's okay. It's kind of a remnant of the old me.

Judith: It's familiar.

Roger: Yes, it's small, there's no negative feeling about it. It's just a little remembrance. I'm not sure if others see me as changed as I feel.

Judith: What does that mean? Have other people seen you as freer and happier than you've been?

Roger: I don't think that they knew I was in as bad a shape as I was at the time. So others can't see how big a change I've made.

Judith: I see.

Roger: But I have talked to other people, Mary, for example, who is just now finding out who I am. She had a whole different image of who I was. And even people I have just met recently say, "Gee, you project one image, but you're really different than that." It's now come to more of a balance where I've got, like, my office kind of personality and my social personality. But I can see that is changing to where they will be one personality, and that will be all the time. I'm not two different people. I'm only one person who is changing.

Judith: Is the difference along some of the lines that we've talked about—that open image or the one that is more serious, quiet, maybe a touch depressed?

Roger: Staid, reserved, controlled—structured.

Judith: Okay, and the other one is freer, looser, happier . . .

Roger: Yeah, exactly, exactly.

Judith: It seems that things are falling into place nicely for you. You have come a long way.

By mentioning his progress, she sets the tone for review.

Roger: Yeah, I find at certain times, like at this party—did you ever watch "The Hulk" on TV? It was sort of Dr. Jeckyll-Mr. Hyde, but in a comic book form. I found myself many times in the middle of that transition, so there's a conflict of two different kinds of personalities operating at the same time. I've moving over toward the more positive approach.

My boss is having some trouble with the change. It's very hard for him to take. That's why I sent him the article. It says that one of the professional ballplayers was talking about every time he watches his son play Little League and his son strikes out or drops the ball, the father gets very upset. He says, "My God, I've played professional baseball for years and I can't tell you how many times I did that myself, but when I did, it didn't bother me at all. But when my son does it, I really get upset." That's the whole idea of putting things in perspective. That's the problem of one of my bosses right now. He made a ton of mistakes in his career, but he gets very upset when anybody else makes a mistake.

Judith: Well, I suspect that the other thing is that he has used his power to intimidate, to maintain his power, and apparently that isn't working very well on you anymore.

Roger: Well, it's working so poorly that even last night he was at the party and I was dragging him around saying, "Come on, how about you having dinner here," rather than waiting for him to give me instructions as boss to employee. The more unnerving that is to him, the more I enjoy it [laughing].

Roger appropriately shows off his newfound confidence.

Judith: It's not all that surprising [she laughs, too].

Together they savor and relish the growth that has taken place.

Roger: A lot of things are changing. I'm not looking forward to winter and the snow, but I'm not afraid of it like I was before, really concerned.

Judith: Well, Roger, even though we're officially ending, that doesn't mean you can never speak to me again if you want to.

She sets the stage for the open-door policy.

Roger: I know that.

Judith: You know, I've considered this our official ending in terms of any regular appointments, but I expect to be around. If either anything terribly difficult or terribly wonderful happens, it's fine to let me know.

Roger: I will do that. I expect to see your picture on the cover of *Psychology Today* . . .

Judith: Oh, sure!

Roger: . . . or something else very special.

Judith: Oh, what a nice vote of confidence [laughing]!

Roger: Sure, I figure that anybody who has enough ability to see me through my problems has got to be pretty smart—creative. So I don't think that's beyond expectations. It's been a great relationship, it really has. Really a positive one. I've very appreciative because I have a basis of comparison. I went to a psychiatrist for six months and he almost drove me crazy. [They both laugh.] Because there weren't any practical answers. "Tell me about that" went on and on and on—it took six months before I had any confidence to tell him anything that was very intimate, and here I can go out the door and try something. I've got some way to experiment. That's

However, she might be leaving the door a bit too open out of her own need. It's important not to convey that he might not do well, especially out of the therapist's anxiety about ending.

Mutual respect and admiration.

incredibly important for me. To see some positive result and say, "Hey, this works," or "She knows what she's talking about."

I should have made some notes about certain words that were used. I don't know whether it's part of therapists' domain to have certain words that they use or become attached to, there were certain words that turned situations around—courage was one—from negative thinking or questionable kind of thinking to very positive thinking. Not being patronizing because that would have been very suspect. But we talked about courage or bravery, that kind of thing, and to me they were very important words. They really gave me a new perspective, a new viewpoint. I should have made a list of those words. They were good words to remember in talking to other people.

Judith obviously used a therapeutic approach founded on health and affirmation.

Judith: Well, that's interesting, Roger, because I can think of a couple of possibilities when I don't think I was all that aware of what those particular words might have been, that had so much meaning to you.

Roger: I've assimilated those words. They were very important at the time and they'd be meaningful to anybody, not just to me.

He refers to her words that were reflective, empathic, and understanding, and

Judith: I can think of one word that I don't think was in your vocabulary at all—anger.

Roger: It's still in lowercase letters [laughs].

Judith: Okay.

Roger: Yeah, I do get angry, maybe I mask it, but it's okay for me to express my anger more directly. I'm not afraid of dealing with this emotion like I was in the past.

Judith: It sounds like you are doing much, much better in expressing your anger in general.

Roger: Oh, by the way, I think our divorce is final. I haven't seen the papers, but . . . [both laugh].

Judith: Incidentally [laughing]?

Roger: Incidentally, yeah.

Judith: You didn't have to go to court or anything?

Roger: No, I don't know where I was that day. I must have been at the office or something, but my attorney showed up in court. I had signed the papers previously.

Judith: Did you get everything worked out so you don't have to have a regular . . .

Roger: Trial?

Judith: Yeah, you know, where the

which enabled him to heal and change. Therapist reminds him gently and humorously of a difficult area. This sets up a review and discussion of work to continue by himself.

It seems that many patients end their treatments around times of external partings. Whether healthy functioning or acting out, it happens frequently. Perhaps there is a need to show one's independent self.

judge ends up deciding settlements and stuff.

Roger: Well, it was pretty simple, as a matter of fact. The night before the final court date was Richard's birthday, so I brought the divorce papers over to the house and had birthday cake. [Both laugh.]

Judith: Was that as easy as you make it sound?

Roger: Yeah, it was. So you can see how far I've come on that one.

Judith: I can hardly believe it—that you would just do that.

Roger: Yeah, well, just to give you an insight into my personality, I was supposed to sign the papers and leave them there for Cathy to sign. Freud would have a good time with this, but I took all the papers home with me without signing them. I didn't realize it until I got back to the apartment. So I called Cathy and said, "Yeah, I forgot. What time are you leaving for court in the morning?" So I signed the papers and in the morning jogged over with the envelope, and kept on with my jogging. Also, I thought you might want to know that I told my mother-in-law off as well.

Judith: This isn't just the termination of therapy—this is a revolution!

She rejoices with him about the changes he has made, especially

Roger: I thought I was going to be emotional. I thought there would be a real tear-jerking parting of the ways. It didn't happen. I said to Cathy, "Here are the papers. It's been fun."

Judith: Because your relationship with her has settled into a different place from a while earlier?

Roger: It just became so evident that we're not on the same wave-length. We're not operating the same at all.

Judith: How did the settlement work out? The reason I'm asking is that you had said quite firmly that you were not going to be taken advantage of. Are you satisfied?

Roger: I think reasonably satisfied. I have a lot less anger and frustration, whatever, than I had before. Where it seemed like I wanted to match everything dollar for dollar, emotion for emotion, I felt it was a reasonable settlement and I just wanted to be parted. I was not going to put everything on one of those scales from the Hall of Justice where everything is balanced.

Judith: The main thing I was interested in was that you did feel okay about it, satisfied with it. Compared to that sense of having been, sort of, taken advantage of before.

regarding the major themes he has worked on.

Even in the final hour, she still affirms his progress and contrasts his new behavior

Roger: I think that for whatever reason Cathy still responds with a certain degree of fear or intimidation about when I get very insistent on something. You know I've begged her to tell me if she is unhappy or upset or disturbed with anything that I do. I mean, I have literally pleaded, and she can't do it. Well, how in the hell am I supposed to know, how am I supposed to guess? So I just go on my merry way and if she can tell me, fine. If she can't, there's nothing I can do about it.

Judith: That's right.

Roger: I don't know of any time when I've actually been really pleased with somebody. I feel frustrated that I can't get satisfaction, but I can accept this even if I don't like it.

Judith: It's great that you can tell the difference—accept it without having to like it.

Roger: I guess the worst thing for me is to get no response.

Judith: That kind of dismissal makes you feel invisible, not validated.

Roger: Invisible or not worthy. You can't get what you want out of a rock.

and feelings to his pretreatment functioning. She does an excellent job of not opening up new issues, which can be an unconscious maneuver by therapists that may confuse clients by planting seeds of doubt about termination.

Judith: Isn't it ironic that the missed appointment—this one—does happen to coincide with the divorce being final? Even though I still would agree that the emotional divorce has already taken place. Really, Roger, when I think about it, it's been a long haul for you and me.

Roger: It's been two-and-a-half years.

Judith: Well, when I think of it in terms of what all has happened—the changes and the growing and struggling—it's been a long, bumpy path.

Roger: It has really been an incredible experience, real incredible. Sometimes I wish that I had videotaped some of the sessions although I don't know if I could stand seeing them again.

Judith: I think that if we had a picture or tape from early on, when we started to meet, just the two of us, to the last few times, there would be an enormous difference. Not only in *what* you're saying—just the way you look and talk. It would come through.

Roger: Well, it's something I've talked about with someone I'm dating, that it's the right time and the right place. Two years ago, it may have been a whole different story.

She brings them back to the theme of ending and loss.

Because, as you say, I'm a different person because of things I'm interested in and do and enjoy.

Judith: I said before that I thought your determination and your ability to hang in there was one more asset, but there's another piece of you that I've just plain enjoyed and that's the sort of creative side. That has come through. I've really appreciated that about you.

She honestly affirms some of his strengths. Even if the total treatment experience has not been as good as this one, there are always positive comments to make.

Roger: You know, I've enjoyed it myself. I really have. It's like a special talent that I have and enjoy using.

Judith: I think the image is the most graphic aspect you have, a sort of creative flair that comes through in a lot of things. Maybe it's the way you think about certain things—that has a very nice creative touch to it.

Roger: It's interesting that sometimes talents or abilities or things that you enjoy, you don't realize you enjoy them until you give them a chance. What moves to mind is that you're not directing me or pushing me in a direction. You're letting me find it. That's much more satisfying.

The client speaks of what factors, processes, or qualities facilitated his growth.

Judith: Are you going to miss coming in or have we strung out these appointments far enough that it isn't going to seem like such an abrupt change?

She brings them back to termination and the feelings involved.

Roger: No, I don't think it will be an abrupt change. There are two things. One, when I was really down, I'd say, "Gee, it would be nice if I had an appointment with Judith to talk about this—hell, I can solve this problem myself." Not that you couldn't help me. I really can solve the problem myself and I did end up solving it. The only negative aspect is why can't I write myself a check for the same amount of money as I do coming here and put it in a savings account? I don't have that much willpower. I've got to figure out a way to do that.

Judith: Well, everything you say seems to point to our time frame being right on target.

Roger: I feel very much at peace and very, very content.

Judith: It's also like a whole lot of things have been resolved.

Roger: I think the things that are important to me are going in a positive way and the things that are unimportant are just sort of pushed out of the picture. They don't have a serious effect on me. If I don't get along with my boss every day of the week, it doesn't make any difference. The real thing that's important is how the Center is doing. What does the financial statement look like? What are my relationships with other people on the job?

Gradual tapering—he has time to experience difficulties and work out solutions, knowing the therapist is still there.

He has internalized the therapeutic work.

Those are the important things.
The other stuff I don't worry about.
I think that before, those things
that were important and unimportant got equal attention. Now they
don't.

Something that came across
in another session we had was what
things are and what things people
perceive they are. That struck me as
being a very important distinction.
If the job is lousy but people think
it's great, what the hell difference
does it make, as long as they think
it's fine and they're satisfied. Why
do you have to turn the whole
world around to what your sense of
feeling is? Why impose your sensi-
tivities? So that's important—to not
try to change the world around for
everybody else.

Judith: That's true of a lot of
things besides your job.

Roger: Richard and Debbie are terrific, just great! They've grown at
least two feet over the summer. I
think they're on their way. Things
are looking great. I haven't gotten
any more money than I had before,
probably less, but that's not important to me.

Perhaps a meta-
phor for his own
growth and
change.

Judith: Apparently you can have
the quality of life that you want.

Roger: Absolutely, absolutely. It's
people, it's all in people, not dollars. I'm very happy with a lot of

the people I've met. I even restarted a relationship with Mary. Remember Mary?

Judith: Yes, I remember Mary [laughing].

Roger: Whole different ballgame, different relationship. The sun does not rise and set on Mary.

Judith: It's really quite a joy to hear what you have to say today. And I surely do wish you well, Roger.

Roger: I have so much confidence and I'm thinking so positively that I just don't see any way it could not go well. I can't see any dark clouds on the horizon, although I know there'll always be problems.

Judith: You sound like you're feeling so good and very confident about the future.

Roger: I think a part of it is to try to anticipate. I have an image of waves coming out on the beach. You have a choice—when the big wave comes in, do you want to stand there and get bowled over, or do you want to step aside and get out on the next piece of the ocean? So, I think there can be bad things, as long as you don't just stand there and let them bowl you over.

Judith: Well, I think what you said is fortuitous. One of the most important things is that even

Even in the last moments, she affirms growth. What is obviously not present is the adherence to the analytic axiom of interpreting until the final minute.

though we have no guarantees we won't have troubles, we have some confidence in ourselves. Then, when something negative comes along, we'll probably figure out how to get ourselves out of it. I think that's the main trick.

Roger: That's the problem-solving ability. Once you solve the first small problem, the sense of self-accomplishment, confidence, just continues to build.

Judith: I will really miss you.

Roger: Thanks for telling me that. You are a very special person and I will never forget you.

Therapist expresses genuine feelings of warmth, which allows the client to do the same.

This is a good example of a positive last session. One difficulty in endings is highlighted by the fact that the client actually missed the original final session—a possible "Freudian slip" or parapraxis. By doing this, he appeared to be expressing some ambivalence toward or avoidance of the bittersweet feelings of saying goodbye. The therapist does an excellent job of not making manipulative interpretations about the missed appointment. It is clear that she supports his decision to terminate and encourages him to come in "so we can kind of wrap it up." She appears to structure the session just enough, avoiding the temptation to open new issues or point out unresolvable ones. She takes each opportunity to support and affirm Roger's changes, growth, and nearly formed self structure. In addition, she gently but directly encourages him to express some of his sad feelings about saying goodbye, using self-disclosure and metaphors.

There is nothing dramatic about this session. The work has already been done during the two-and-a-half years of therapy. It seems clear that the core characteristics Judith displays, such as warmth, genuineness, empathy, and self-disclosure, have been present during the entire treatment. Without these, a positive and productive final session most likely would not have occurred. I disagree with Samuel Lipton (1961) and others who claim that a cold and mechanistic neutrality adds to a positive therapeutic experience and enhances a treatment ending. According to Lipton's article "The Last Hour," the analytic process should be continued to the very end with the analyst holding steadfastly to the rules of neutrality and free association, not just in the "last hour" but in the last minute as well (p. 325).

Lipton warns practitioners to be careful of "patients who so frequently look forward to some form of transference gratification at the conclusion and tend to use this period as an important enclave for fantasies" (p. 325). After more than four years and seven hundred hours in a treatment relationship he uses as an illustration, Lipton writes that it is inappropriate for the patient, in the final moments, to express gratitude and warmth. After his patient voiced such feelings, Lipton steers him back to his own agenda—maintaining the analytic process to the end. "Thoughts about his relationship with me came up and he said he would miss coming and appreciated what I had done. I suggested that he return to the element of the dream" (p. 329).

Earlier Lipton reports that the patient's primary defense was isolation and a difficulty expressing positive affect or closeness. Therefore, this patient's remarks should have been mirrored with warmth to affirm his progress and growth. Instead, the clinician goes back to the dream, the terrain with which he is most comfortable. I do not view this process as neutral or nondirective. It seems inhuman not to say goodbye, express some feelings, or allow the patient to do so without interpreting this natural reaction as something negative. Rigidly adhering to the principles of which Lipton speaks can also be interpreted as the therapist avoiding the end of treatment, with all its accompanying feelings and problems. The affectionate affirmation that the therapist Judith offers in the final session is the appropriate, satisfying, positive, human manner in which a treatment relationship should terminate.

8

Guidelines for Positive Therapeutic Endings

The goal in this chapter is to propose suggested guidelines about the ending phase in treatment and offer a foundation on which clinicians may structure termination in their own practices.

Generally, it appears that practitioners of psychotherapy, even experienced and well-trained ones, lack knowledge of the important ending process. When clients ask how long treatment will last or how they will know when it is finished, many therapists answer such questions vaguely or arbitrarily, if they answer at all. An unhelpful response or a less-than-forthright discussion of this issue may encourage clients to act out in order to bring the therapy to an end. However, before clinicians can discuss the length, process, and ending of treatment, they themselves must first be more clear about these issues.

Guidelines for Satisfactory Endings

As discussed in prior chapters, many factors converge to make termination either growth-promoting for patients or an iatrogenic experience. To a large extent, the crucial variables are within the control of the practitioner. Some of these variables, which are discussed below, include understanding the limitations of treatment, formulating realistic and obtainable goals, educating clients, being aware of countertransference issues, maintaining empathy, discussing termination early, reviewing treatment, keeping the door open, watching for termination cues, and respecting clients' autonomy.

Accept Limitations of Treatment. One of the first steps therapists can take toward satisfactory terminations is to come to terms with the limitations of treatment. To do this, it is necessary to pull away from some of the negative influences of classical psychoanalysis such as focusing exclusively on psychopathology and striving for perfectionistic outcome. This process has already begun in the field of psychotherapy. New techniques and theoretical approaches flourish and there is movement toward integrating and synthesizing various theories. The term "psychoanalytically informed," which has recently become popular, implies that practitioners can take some important elements of the classical analytic approach and use them to comprehend a general view of human behavior rather than to actually structure treatment. For instance, a therapist may acknowledge and accept the concept of the unconscious or of transference, but not use it as a primary guiding principle in a once- or twice-a-week psychotherapy. Psychotherapy does not cure nor is it the solution to all of life's problems. Clinicians need to guard against both a myopic and a grandiose view.

Educate Clients. Practitioners must work with clients to formulate obtainable treatment goals: Help them understand that cure, change, and growth are relative rather than absolute. Discuss termination in the early stage of treatment and throughout the course of therapy. Let the client know about the inherent difficulty of determining when treatment is finished. It is important to bring the formerly covert, nonverbal termination process into the open where it can be candidly discussed instead of acted out by both client and therapist.

Be Aware of Countertransference Issues. Another significant way clinicians can improve the termination process is to monitor their feelings of countertransference so that personal emotions do not interfere with the ending of treatment relationships. Therapists' emotional and economic dependence upon their patients appear to be of such profound importance that without special attention, these narcissistic issues will continue to obstruct positive psychotherapy outcomes.

Some practical suggestions for avoiding countertransference problems in termination include the following:

1. Therapists might attempt to guard against patient loads getting too small; it is dangerous to be overly dependent on a few patients. Actively building a practice and maintaining a stream of new referrals can help ease the unconscious need to hang on for financial reasons.

2. Conversely, practitioners need to avoid becoming so busy that they have no time to reflect on treatment plans. It is very difficult to extend empathy and maintain sensitivity to termination issues if one is overextended.

3. To guard against emotional countertransference, practitioners can try to enjoy the fullest lives possible. Isolated psychotherapists, even when professionally very busy, may be predisposed to being overly dependent upon patients for emotional gratification if their own interpersonal relationships are too sparse. In addition, spending too much time in psychotherapy sessions can encourage a myopic view of life and an overvaluation of treatment. This may produce countertransference feelings relating to issues of enmeshment.

4. Independent practitioners may find it useful to purchase regular or periodic consultation supervision to discuss treatment issues, especially as they relate to ending and letting go.

Distinguish Between Clients' Treatment Goals and Your Own Therapy Aims. The confusion between the goals and expectations of therapists' own treatment and that of their clients is a special type of countertransference that is seldom discussed in the literature. Therapist/patients aspire to gain insight, become as self-aware as possible, develop and maintain a cohesive self structure, and other overly ambitious goals. Most nontherapist psychotherapy consumers, however, hope only to feel better or lessen the problems that originally brought them to therapy.

Practitioners need to maintain a clear distinction between their own interminability as patients (particularly when treatment is a form of continuing education) and their clients' more modest and practical goals. It is true that Freud (1957) called for analysts to be analyzed at five-year intervals; however, he suggested that the average analysis should last six to nine months. Being reanalyzed every five years did not mean that a practitioner would be in treatment continuously and interminably. I do not believe this was Freud's intent. However, if therapists wish to be interminable psychotherapy consumers, that is their choice as long as they do not confuse their own treatment length and depth with that of their clients. If perfectionistic treatment goals are added to therapists' frequently interminable personal treatment, it is no mystery why they may have a difficult time with their patients' treatment endings.

Rigid, dogmatic models that "apply" to all patients are dangerous in any case. Fearing the effect that training analyses have on the creativity of the analysand, let alone a lifetime of analysis, Kohut (1984) wrote: "What of the analysts who show evidence of true intellectual independence and creative enterprise? And omitting issues of native and early acquired talent (a large omission indeed!) and restricting our focus to the influence of the training analyses, what accounts for the fact that these analysts, braving the disapproval of the large majority of their colleagues who are sustained by the maintenance of the scientific status quo, will think new thoughts and point out new ways of achieving scientific goals" (p. 168). I think Kohut would share my concern about the overanalyzed practitioner who was not encouraged to develop his or her creative potential and separate self even if it differed markedly from the traditional view of the treating therapist. Describing the end of a long analytic treatment, one of Kohut's therapist/clients said to him: "Now I am similar to you only in one respect: I am an independent person just like you" (p. 169). This should be the basic tenet for all treatment experiences, whether the patient is a therapist or a lay person. Clones produce more clones, reinforcing dogma. Independent individuals produce unique and creative approaches to psychopathology and to life's problems.

Maintain Empathy. When clinicians maximize the use of empathy (as defined by Rogers and his followers and by Kohut and his followers), then the numerous countertransference issues that obstruct the ending process will be minimized. Such termination problems are more apt to develop when there is a break in the empathic bond between client and therapist. Maintaining empathy is monumentally important as a precondition for treatment as well as the most vital "curative" or change factor in all stages of psychotherapy. Whether used for accurate assessment/diagnosis, for treatment, or for the letting go of treatment, it is essential to a positive psychotherapy experience.

At various points in prior chapters, the concept of empathy as espoused by client-centered or self psychology theorists has been discussed and contrasted. The greater contrast is between these two schools and classical analytic practitioners who use interpretation even in the last moments of treatment and are overly focused on applying rigid theory instead of helping clients to understand the meaning of ending. These differences have been described in many case examples.

Empathy is also related to the issue of fees. Again, comparing schools of thought, Raskin and Rogers (1989) report that client-centered/humanistic practitioners should negotiate fees with clients. This school of thought recognizes that feelings about money tend to be intense in this society and that they may affect clients' self structures. Therapists who adhere to the classical analytical approach set the fee and make the decisions as to how payment will be handled. My research indicates that mismanagement of the issue of fees results in irreparable damage to therapist-client relations and can often result in negative terminations.

Discuss Termination Early. The literature and my research and observations strongly indicate that clinicians generally wait for clients to initiate the ending of psychotherapy. Since this is the case, it would seem logical to say to clients at the beginning of treatment something like "I will wait for you to tell me when you are ready to talk about ending your therapy." Clients then have the option of discussing the subject at the onset. The point of doing this is not only to inform but also to encourage an early interchange about termination. Clients may say they are not equipped to end therapy, that the therapist is the expert. Or they may readily understand and agree, but not wish to pursue the matter at that point.

Practitioners who prefer mutual and simultaneous initiation of termination—which seems virtually impossible since someone needs to verbalize the issue first—may want to use a statement such as this: "I believe that when we are ready to finish our work together, we both should agree and feel ready to end." Even such a basic, explicit statement by the therapist in the early stage of treatment is a preliminary step toward promoting a dialogue and thus structuring a shadowy process.

Review Treatment. A review of treatment was considered important by most of the therapists I interviewed. By review they mean a planned or spontaneous discussion of where clients started compared with where they are at the conclusion of treatment in terms of presenting problems, life difficulties, interpersonal relationships, transference issues, and other aspects of change and growth. This review and summing-up process should include discussion of how to maintain treatment gains as well as areas clients can continue to work on by themselves after treatment ends.

Clinicians who prefer a definite structuring of the last session or sessions may purposely include a recapitulation of treatment, particularly if they believe that discussing clients' progress and gains is significant for lasting change. Practitioners who prefer to follow the clients' lead and not interfere with autonomous functioning will be more comfortable reacting and responding instead of directing, thus taking the chance that the treatment review will either emerge spontaneously or not occur at all.

Keep the Door Open. Termination with a raincheck or the open-door policy is another important concept that deserves some elaboration because of its popularity among practitioners. There appear to be two primary methods in use. One is to assure clients that they may return for treatment at any time and not emphasize the end as a distinct process. The other method also involves assuring clients about the therapists' availability, but also focuses on officially ending treatment. This approach, which I prefer, enables both clients and clinicians to obtain a certain closure, which is essential for continued human growth and development. To keep the door open without saying goodbye may be a way of avoiding the bittersweet emotions that are a normal part of termination. Saying goodbye allows both parties to address the difficult business of leave-taking and frees the client to move forward.

Both types of open-door policy imply a belief in treatment as an ongoing, evolutionary process, a belief in relative rather than absolute cure, and a commitment to the basic pragmatism of remaining sensitive to clients' changing needs.

Observe Termination Cues. Therapists need to be sensitive to cues from clients that indicate they are considering termination, even at an unaware level. Such a cue may be that a client has less substantive material to discuss. There are often fewer conflicts and problems to talk about in the sessions prior to initiating termination. This period can be thought of as the inception of the formal termination process, even though it frequently is not recognized as such. Clinicians may tend to overlook termination cues, especially if they affect a valued relationship. The feeling tone of this period is almost a nonverbal calm or lull. How therapists handle treatment at this pivotal point is crucial in determining the remaining course of psychotherapy. Will ending be approached openly or left in the closet, to be acted out at some future point?

Another cue to watch for is the development of a more equitable or peerlike relationship between practitioner and client. This interaction, inseparable from the total gestalt of treatment, is reciprocal, covert, and multidimensional. It may mean the client neither idealizes nor depreciates the therapist, but views him or her as a human being with good and bad qualities. In classical analytic language this phenomenon is described as "resolution of the transference." Humanistic theorists would say the client has "developed a more genuine self." This change in relationship also affects practitioners who begin to relate to clients, perhaps at times unconsciously, in a more candid, less formal fashion. Many therapists increase their self-disclosure, either spontaneously or according to a plan. They may find that clients require less evaluation, support, and interpretation as termination nears. This equalization is natural in a positive treatment experience.

Clinicians need to recognize this change in relationship and then reflect and affirm it. Repeatedly, and in a variety of ways, they should make statements such as "It's really fine to see you feeling so good and figuring things out more and more on your own. I remember when that would have been too difficult for you. It seems you need less and less feedback from me." What previously had been part of the dyadic interaction becomes slowly but progressively internalized by the client. Although each individual needs good self-objects at all stages of life, the urgency and intensity of the need for the therapist lessens as the self structure becomes healthy toward the end of treatment.

Another cue signaling that termination may be at hand is a gradual decrease in session frequency. This does not mean an occasional missed appointment, but a continual progressive pattern. Once-a-week clients may begin to come in biweekly or three times a month; twice-a-week clients may start to cancel once a week. These alterations of schedule are not usually conscious adjustments to the ending stage; consequently clients are unlikely to state their intent to come in less often and may not be aware that they are weaning themselves from treatment. Therapists also may not recognize what is happening, but reduction of the number of sessions usually draws their attention. Connected to fewer sessions is the client's decreasing need for input, evaluation, and interpretation as termination approaches. Discussions become less substantive as clients cope more effectively, thus signaling the end of treatment.

A key to helping clients structure reasonable and productive endings is to make every effort to minimize the termination countertransference issues when ending cues surface. A balanced response is essential: It needs to be empathic as well as flexible. Meeting the client's termination needs may require some personal sacrifice on the part of the clinician, especially one who is somewhat rigid regarding fees and scheduling. This was brought home to me early in my practice when a client gave me strong cues by frequently rescheduling appointments. I was annoyed by the inconvenience to my schedule and began acting out feelings about the termination rather than working them through. I learned from this difficult ending that my precious schedule may need to be interrupted once in a while, especially to accommodate a positive termination.

Practitioners should become sensitive to such cues and ask clients whether they are having thoughts or feelings about termination. If this is a conscious issue, the therapist's verbal expression will initiate discussions and plans for the ending process. If the clients' intentions to terminate are unconscious, discussion may stimulate thoughts and feelings behind the observed changes in session frequency, session content, client-therapist relationship, or other cues. Such a probe can bring to the fore problems that have not yet been worked on or revitalize a stagnating psychotherapy. However, observable cues need not be used to the exclusion of a more intuitive approach. The integration of these two techniques makes good clinical sense.

Respect Clients' Autonomy. When the client initiates termination and the clinician disagrees, or vice versa, termination may present many problems. Especially troublesome are cases in which the client wants to end but the therapist feels he or she is "not ready" because of unresolved problems that need further work. Often a client's desire to end treatment is interpreted by the therapist as acting out, thus adding more confusion to this already complex process. The important matter of viewing the client as a self-directed human being can be lost during such a struggle. Many therapists express their great respect for the client's autonomy, but find ways to obstruct the person's independence. For example, an experienced practitioner told me, "It is terrible that some therapists use interpretation as manipulation to try to keep patients in treatment longer than they might want to be." However, in describing a recent termination, he told me that the client's desire to end psychotherapy was "premature" and "a form of resistance." When it comes to ending the treatment relationship, what clinicians theorize and what they actually practice are often quite different.

If a therapist truly believes that the client's attainment of self-directiveness is a guiding principle of psychotherapy, then the client's decision to terminate must always be respected. The following vignette illustrates how I almost forgot this principle. Mary K. was referred to me by her physician because of "strange" behavior, which included repeating certain "bizarre" phrases. The referring neurologist ruled out organic factors. My assessment was that the patient was psychotically depressed; she appeared to be functioning at a minimal level. I felt she might be kept out of the hospital with individual psychotherapy and possibly the use of medication.

She came to treatment once a week and made remarkable progress. Within three months, she was feeling and functioning even more fully than prior to the onset of her problems. Ms. K. then started to make termination noises, which startled me because just a short time ago her psychopathology was so severe that hospitalization had been seriously considered. She asked how much longer she would need to attend sessions and if it was necessary to continue to come in so often. I was amazed because I actually felt she should be coming in more often than once a week. Before I could think this through, words slipped out of my mouth that uncomfortably resembled the countertransference-laden remarks I so dislike when other therapists use them. I said something like, "How can you be considering stopping therapy so soon when you have been so ill and are now doing so well?"

I could see in her eyes an expression of bewilderment because until then I had been extremely affirming of her change and growth. She was obviously quite taken aback to hear me expressing doubts and warnings about her mental health. Fortunately for both of us, I instantly saw the danger signals and immediately attempted to correct my mistake. I assured her that she could try coming in less often to determine how she felt. Moreover, I reaffirmed that I would help her end therapy as much as I had helped her begin it. Ms. K. then tapered her sessions and soon terminated in a manner with which *she* was comfortable. This patient only wanted to feel better again, and when this began to happen it was natural for her to think about ending therapy. Of course, it was also natural for me to be cautious and conservative because of my training to be aware of "flights into health," which encouraged a tendency to underestimate people's will and strength. My mistake was to burden my client with my concerns.

Ms. K. had done what she set out to do. With that accomplished, she wanted to get out of treatment and put the conflicts behind her. She was not an insight-oriented individual and would not have sought out psychotherapy if she had not been in a crisis state. If I had not recovered relatively rapidly from my error, I could have undone a great deal of hard work (on both our parts) with the honest intent of ensuring her continued progress. What a paradox!

It was respect for the client's goals and needs that enabled the successful treatment experience to end in a positive manner. It may be that the more severe the patient's initial psychopathology, the less time is taken at the start to educate him or her about treatment, discuss the ending process, or set agreed-upon goals. When the patient starts to improve, the therapist should offer some structure and perspective, following the suggestions given earlier for educating clients.

Because a clinician adheres to the guiding principle of self-directiveness does not mean that he or she cannot continue to comment or express opinions; but such offerings are different from interpretations designed to control the client or to persuade the client to accept the clinician's viewpoint. There is a fine line between feedback that offers a divergent opinion and feedback that tries to manipulate. If the therapist does not agree with the client's wish to terminate, he or she might say something like this: "You have come a long way. You have reached some of your goals, but not others. In my opinion there is still more to work on, but a therapist frequently wants to do more. However, I strongly believe that people must take responsibility for themselves, so I will respect your decision and help you end therapy as I helped you begin."

It is essential to verbalize these ideas, but if the practitioner does not feel them and mean them authentically, they will have little impact or power for the client. Even more fundamental, as emphasized in earlier chapters, is the need for meaning and process of ending treatment to be discussed throughout the entire therapy, not just at the final stage.

Whether they are laypeople or therapists, clients strive to be independent and free-acting beings. A number of interviewed individuals were adamant about not feeling their freedom and autonomy until they had terminated. One practitioner's statement about her personal treatment was echoed by many others: "It was important for me to terminate and feel I could make it on my own in spite of my therapist's disagreement regarding my readiness for terminating. That fact that I could still end, even though he disagreed, proved to me I really was ready."

Of extreme importance is that clinicians should avoid placing clients in "catch-22" predicaments. Examples of these are replete in the literature as well as in clinical practice. Ferenczi (1955 [1927]) felt that a client's desire to terminate analysis indicated that the person was hiding something neurotic. This is a no-win situation for the client, whose feelings are never respected and, in fact, are used as evidence against his or her readiness for termination. It is classical analytic thinking at its worst, especially as it relates to ending psychotherapy. To receive the therapist's blessing with regard to terminating, the client may have to behave like Br'er Rabbit in the briar patch and say, "I never want to end my psychotherapy—please let me come forever!"

New Beginnings

This final case illustration, from my own treatment experience, is similar to Rossner's fictional situation (described in Chapter Four) in that the main client character was extremely concerned about dependency issues that made the therapy complex and the termination process sensitive.

Like many psychotherapy patients seen in large metropolitan areas, Ms. Inez C. was a professional, doing well in her career but unhappy about her personal life. She was mildly to moderately depressed and had been unable to become interdependently and intimately involved with a man. Her outward attractiveness and effervescent personality masked her low self-esteem. In early childhood, her life had been totally disrupted when her mother was killed in an accident. To survive psychologically, she developed some compensatory self structures that served her well at times. Now, forming a trusting, lasting relationship was both appropriate and desirable, but the structures developed in her early life were apparently thwarting her development. In the course of her psychotherapy with me, which lasted three-and-a-quarter years, this patient made outstanding progress. She accomplished what she set out to do. She grew psychologically, increasing her sense of self and becoming free to choose a mate who complemented her.

It was not easy for Ms. C. to come for treatment, stay in treatment, or to end it in a healthy fashion. From her initial phone call, the related themes of commitment, interdependency, trust, and loss were present and formed the focal point of the therapeutic process. Understandably, she always wanted to leave before she was left, and she entered relationships slowly and extremely tentatively. She spoke in the early sessions of being concerned about becoming overly dependent on the therapist, a theme that was present throughout the treatment to varying degrees.

Very slowly, Ms. C. began to develop a more cohesive self structure. She was able to trust and depend on me more, learning not just intellectually but emotionally that she needed to depend on someone first before she could actually feel more independent and secure with her self. The termination process began slowly and subtly. Although we dealt repeatedly with the theme of endings, and specifically the end of treatment, there began to be a budding, healthy quality to the issue. It was no longer the verbalization of a child threatening to leave to avoid being hurt. She sounded increasingly like a young adult who was considering moving on, and in a sense moving out—of my office, our place to her place.

I fully realized my immense responsibility to give her exactly what she needed—not too much or too little. If I moved too quickly or too abruptly into ending the therapy, she could easily feel rushed out and not valued, which could have destroyed much good work. On the other hand, if she suggested terminating and I disagreed, directly or subtly, she could have perceived me holding her back, giving her messages that she was not healthy enough to leave. Certainly, any such verbal or nonverbal communication would have had a deleterious effect on both the treatment process and the ending process.

I tried over time to give the same communication in many different ways: "You showed courage and fortitude before entering therapy. In treatment you have matured and grown, and it has been an honor to work with you. We will say goodbye in a manner and at a rate that makes you comfortable. It hurts much more over the course of a lifetime to stay isolated and detached from other human beings than it does to risk loss."

She heard my message and felt its authenticity, and the tapering off process commenced. It was one of the slowest termination stages I have participated in; it took more than a year—and the slowness was extremely important to the patient. The amount of time between sessions was not typical;

sometimes there was an interval of two or three months. What is significant is that the client's pace was being respected.

It would be useful to hear what Ms. C. had to say about this termination. Here is part of a note she gave me:

Letting go has always been a problem for me and was interfering in many areas of my life. It was no surprise to me that it was an issue in therapy. For quite some time, I have been bringing up the need to terminate. Many factors influenced my feelings that I should stop. Money was one. Some feelings of guilt about still coming was another. Also, I felt sometimes that I wasn't "crazy," so why did I need a therapist? At any rate, I continued with sessions because I felt in spite of all these other things I still was getting a lot out of it.

When and how did I finally decide to stop? Over a period of time my sessions have become less of a major focus in my life. When I began therapy, I lived for my sessions. Now I still enjoy the time but attend less regularly and at times almost feel that I don't really want to make the drive. I used to feel that the sessions were not really long enough to say all I wanted. Now, though I attend less, I rarely have a burning issue to discuss. Also, in the last year numerous major crises have occurred, some especially concerning connecting and loss which I felt I handled extremely well, basically on my own. I didn't have the same need to check out what I was doing with you.

Knowing and feeling all of these things, I still did not really want to end my sessions. I remember after a session thinking about my feelings of dependency on therapy and explaining to a friend that it was the only place I could find unconditional acceptance. I realized that, not in the beginning of therapy when I wasn't capable of asking for much from others, but now it was kind of a cop-out—I was using this as an excuse because as long as I never ask friends, family, husband, for this acceptance, I can never get it. Therefore, I was in a way

using therapy as an excuse not to progress even farther
in my relationships.

It also makes me feel good to know I can return if
I want to. Endings don't always have to be permanent
and sudden as they have been in my life.

A neglected theme in many treatments is the desire—
expressed by this patient—to hang onto therapy partly to
avoid life's risks. It is understandable to cling to the known,
especially when it is safe and secure. The therapist must try
to be sensitive to the presence of this phenomena, not to
create it where it does not exist or to neglect it when it is
present, even at a subtle level. When Ms. C. left treatment, I
was as sad and happy as she was. The bittersweet feelings of
endings and new beginnings were present for both of us.

Suggestions for Further Inquiries

This book is not intended to be the ultimate prescription for
the complex termination process. It is an attempt to generate
some hypotheses about the ending process of psychotherapy
as well as to offer guidelines for terminating in clinical practice. Following are a few suggestions for other investigators
to build on the findings presented in this work.

Subsequent inquiries regarding the end of treatment
might expand some of the guidelines by comparing and contrasting client and clinician views of termination on a larger
scale than the research conducted by me for this book did.
Future investigators might also explore whether extratreat-
ment variables such as a patient's divorce, death of a loved
one, and client or therapist absence from treatment may be
related to the initiation of termination. An ideal study design
might be one that collects data from clients and therapists
both at the beginning and at the end of treatment. In this
way it would be possible to assess factors of the interaction
between therapist and client that affect the termination process. The addition of a pretherapy interview or questionnaire
would allow a specific assessment of client and therapist

expectations regarding termination. Optimally, audiotapes from the onset of therapy through the last session would enable researchers/clinicians to comprehend the nuances involved in this process.

Such a design would also lend itself to experimental manipulation to illuminate some of the issues that have been suggested in this project as particularly significant aspects of termination. For example, one group of therapists could be instructed to talk with clients about specific termination issues at the beginning of therapy and at certain points during treatment. These clients could then be compared to a second group whose therapists have provided no information about ending treatment. As in most experimental investigations of psychotherapy, controlling for other variables is intrinsically difficult. In spite of this problem, an investigation of this type would provide an interesting means of relating awareness and structure of termination to client satisfaction, length of treatment, theoretical orientation, specific criteria, and other variables.

Overall, the goal of subsequent research should be to facilitate the process of termination by developing a coherent, predictable theory and structure that is understood and agreed upon by both clients and therapists at the onset of treatment.

Terminating treatment is difficult but potentially beneficial and growth-promoting for both clients and therapists. As one clinician commented, "The whole dynamic of therapy is captured in the notion of a controlled or limited relationship. The task is one of learning to value relationships that have limits. It is symbolic of learning to value life, time, and death." Thus, as the process of defining the limits of therapy, termination becomes a distillation of all that has preceded it and paves the way for new beginnings. Sue Chance (1987) sums up the end of the treatment relationship when she writes: "Saying goodbye is not a moment, it's a process. It's an echo down canyon walls and into the depths of caves, magically vibrating the air for years and coming back to us in waves, often when we least expect it" (p. 21).

From the inception of each psychotherapeutic experience through the middle phase and on to its conclusion, the basic paradox is present: two people come together to ultimately go separate ways. The therapist must be clear from the first contact, unless there are mitigating circumstances, that the intent of treatment is to help the patient function without the therapist. Along the lengthy road of an open-ended treatment, there are numerous obstacles, some placed there by patients but many by practitioners themselves. However, whether practitioners describe their role as transitional object, good parent, or empathic facilitator, the results—change and growth—are what is important to the termination process.

Resource:
Studies of the Termination Process in Psychotherapy

This book is partially based on the data and results of my 1982 and 1986 studies of the termination practices and theoretical models used by a group of therapists providing long-term, open-ended individual psychotherapy in private practice settings (Kramer, 1986). The general question was "What is the nature of the termination process in open-ended psychotherapy?" The attitudes, values, theories, and opinions of practitioners and clients were explored in an effort to better understand the business of ending psychotherapy in order to achieve more satisfying endings.

The subjects for both studies were chosen using an availability sampling method (Levitt, 1961) in which the researcher identifies a core group of potential subjects who fit the sampling criteria. They are requested to participate in the study and to refer other subjects who fit the criteria. The sampling criteria required the therapists to be engaged in private psychotherapy practice; have clients in open-ended, individual psychotherapy; and be willing to engage in at least two in-depth interviews on the general topic of termination in therapy. This technique inherently limits generalizability, but provides an optimum means of gathering in-depth data in a particular subject area.

167

The sample was actually somewhat diverse within the criteria. The orientation of the subjects was almost equally balanced between psychodynamic, eclectic, and humanistic schools of thought. By intent, the subjects did not include behavioral clinicians, brief psychotherapists, or strictly family therapists, since these are not approaches that practice open-ended, long-term, individual psychotherapy with a self-inter-personal or intrapsychic focus. Both studies also included subjects from the disciplines of psychology, social work, and psychiatry. In the 1982 study twenty clinicians provided their views of psychotherapy termination based on the two most recent endings in their own practices, while those who had also been clients discussed their personal experiences. The 1986 study duplicated the earlier one, but interviewed ten additional psychotherapists and fifteen lay clients.

Although different theoretical orientations, academic backgrounds, and client types are represented, the sample is still somewhat selective. Because of its relatively small size, it does not allow for much interpretation of differences across theoretical orientation or client type. However, it does serve well in providing a means of generating hypotheses and suggesting ideas and concepts about the termination process in open-ended psychotherapy. This holds true for the original study in 1982, the expansion and addition in the 1986 study, and the observations from my clinical experience and supervision of other clinicians over the course of my career.

A personal interview was selected as the primary method to investigate the termination process as opposed to the somewhat more narrow information derived from a questionnaire. It was felt that a semistructured interview would provide for greater depth of information, allow for follow-through on interesting answers, and encourage subjects to discuss their feelings, perceptions, and thoughts regarding psychotherapy endings.

In part, the interview style project was derived from the idea that what people say in answer to a question does reflect how they act out their beliefs when given the opportunity (Ittleson, Proshansky, Rivlin, and Winkel, 1974). Self-disclosure in a nonthreatening environment was the ideal that the interviewer tried to obtain. Subjects were interviewed either in their office or home at their convenience. They were asked to set aside a two-hour block of time for the interview, which was tape-recorded.

References

Alexander, F. "The Dynamics of Psychotherapy in the Light of Learning Theory." *American Journal of Psychiatry*, 1963, *120*, 440.

Applebaum, S. A., and Holzman, P. S. " 'End-Setting' as a Therapeutic Event." *Psychiatry*, 1967, *30* (3), 276–282.

Berenstein, I. "Analysis: Terminable and Interminable, Fifty Years On." *International Journal of Psycho-Analysis*, 1987, *68*, 21–35.

Blanck, G., and Blanck, R. *Ego Psychology: Theory and Practice.* New York: Columbia University Press, 1974.

Blum, H. P. "Analysis Terminable and Interminable: A Half Century Retrospective." *International Journal of Psycho-Analysis*, 1987, *68* (1), 37–47.

Bolen, J. K. "Easing the Pain of Termination for Adolescents." *Social Casework*, Nov. 1972, pp. 519–527.

Buxbaum, E. "Technique of Terminating Analysis." *International Journal of Psycho-Analysis*, 1950, *31*, 184–190.

Cavenar, J., and Nash, J. "The Dream as Signal for Termination." *Journal of the American Psychoanalytic Association*, 1976, *24* (2), 425–436.

Chance, S. "Goodbye Again." *The Psychiatric Time/Medicine and Behavior*, Jan. 1987, pp. 11, 21.

171

Dewald, P. A. *Psychotherapy: A Dynamic Approach.* New York: Basic Books, 1964.

Dewald, P. A. "Reactions to the Forced Termination of Therapy." *Psychiatric Quarterly,* 1965, *39,* 102–126.

Epstein, L. *Helping People: The Task-Centered Approach.* St. Louis: Mosby, 1980.

Ferenczi, S. "Discontinuous Analyses." In J. Richman (ed.), *Further Contributions to the Theory and Technique of Psycho-Analysis.* London: Hogarth Press, 1950. (Originally published 1914.)

Ferenczi, S. "The Problem of Termination of Psychoanalysis." In M. Balint (ed.), *Final Contributions to the Problems and Methods of Psycho-Analysis.* New York: Basic Books, 1955. (Originally published 1927.)

Ferenczi, S., and Rank, O. *The Development of Psychoanalysis.* New York: Dover, 1956. (Originally published 1924.)

Firestein, S. K. *Termination in Psychoanalysis.* New York: International Universities Press, 1978.

Fox, E., Nelson, M., and Bolman, W. "The Termination Process: A Neglected Dimension in Social Work." *Social Work,* 1969, *14* (4), 53–63.

Freud, S. "The Ego and the Id." *The Standard Edition of the Complete Psychological Works of Sigmund Freud.* (J. Strachey, ed. and trans.) Vol. 19. London: Hogarth Press, 1923.

Freud, S. *The Standard Edition of the Complete Psychological Works of Sigmund Freud.* (J. Strachey, ed. and trans.) London: Hogarth Press, 1957.

Freud, S. *Therapy and Technique.* (P. Rieff, ed.) New York: Collier Books, 1963.

Freud, S. "Analysis Terminable and Interminable." In J. Strachey (ed.), *The Standard Edition of the Complete Psychological Works of Sigmund Freud.* Vol. 23. London: Hogarth Press, 1964. (Originally published 1937.)

Fromm-Reichman, F. *Principles of Intensive Psychotherapy.* Chicago: University of Chicago Press, 1950.

Gambrill, E. *Behavior Modification: Handbook of Assessment, Intervention, and Evaluation.* San Francisco: Jossey-Bass, 1978.

Garfield, S. "Research on Client Variables in Psychotherapy." In A. Bergin and S. Garfield (eds.), *Handbook of Psychotherapy and Behavior Change.* New York: Wiley, 1971.

Gaskill, H. "The Closing Phase of the Psychoanalytic Treatment of Adults and the Goals of Psychoanalysis: The Myth of Perfectability." *International Journal of Psycho-Analysis,* 1980, *61,* 10–23.

Gittelson, M. "The Curative Factors in Psychoanalysis in the First Phase of Psychoanalysis." *International Journal of Psycho-Analysis,* 1962, *43,* 194–206.

Glover, E. "The Terminal Phase." In E. Glover, *The Technique of Psycho-Analysis.* New York: International Universities Press, 1955.

Goldberg, A. "Narcissism and the Readiness for Psychotherapy Termination." *Archives of General Psychiatry,* 1975, *32* (6), 695–699.

Gottman, J. M., and Lieblum, S. K. "How to Do Psychotherapy and How to Evaluate It." New York: Holt, Rinehart & Winston, 1974.

Haley, J. *Problem-Solving Therapy: New Strategies for Effective Family Therapy.* San Francisco: Jossey-Bass, 1976.

Hartmann, H. "Psychoanalysis and the Concept of Health." In *Essays on Ego Psychology.* New York: International Universities Press, 1964.

Hollender, M. *The Practice of Psychoanalytic Therapy.* New York: Grune & Stratton, 1965.

Ittleson, W., Proshansky, H., Rivlin, L., and Winkel, G. *An Introduction to Environmental Psychology.* New York: Holt, 1974.

Jahoda, M. *Current Concepts of Positive Mental Health.* New York: Basic Books, 1958.

Jung, C. G. *Modern Man in Search of a Soul.* London: Kegan, Paul, French Trubner, 1945.

Jung, C. G. "Introduction to the Religious and Psychological Problems of Alchemy." In G. Adler and others (eds.), *Collected Works* (R. F. Hull, trans.), Vol. 7: *Psychology and Alchemy.* New York: Pantheon, 1953. (Originally published 1944.)

Jung, C. G. "Principles of Practical Psychotherapy." In G. Adler and others (eds.), *Collected Works* (R. F. Hull, trans.), Vol. 16: *The Practice of Psychotherapy*. New York: Pantheon, 1954a. (Originally published 1935.)

Jung, C. G. "What is Psychotherapy?" In G. Adler and others (eds.), *Collected Works* (R. H. Hull, trans.), Vol. 16: *The Practice of Psychotherapy*. New York: Pantheon, 1954b. (Originally published 1935.)

Jung, C. G. "On the Psychology and Pathology of So Called Occult Phenomena." In G. Adler and others (eds.), *Collected Works* (R. F. Hull, trans.), Vol. 1: *Psychiatric Studies*. Princeton University Press, 1957.

Jung, C. G. "The Archetypes and the Collective Unconscious." In G. Adler and others (eds.), *Collected Works* (R. F. Hull, trans.), Vol. 9: *The Archetypes and the Collective Unconscious*. New York: Pantheon, 1959.

Jung, C. G. "The Transcendent Function." In G. Adler and others (eds.), *Collected Works* (R. F. Hull, trans.), Vol. 8: *The Structure and Dynamic of the Psyche*. New York: Pantheon, 1966. (Originally published 1916.)

Kauff, P. "The Termination Process: Its Relationship to the Separation-Individuation Phase of Development." *International Journal of Group Psychotherapy*, 1977, *27*, 3–18.

Kernberg, O. "Psychotherapy and Psychoanalysis: Final Report of the Menninger Foundation's Psychotherapy Research Project." *Bulletin of the Menninger Clinic*, 1977, *36*.

Klein, M. "On the Criteria for Termination of a Psychoanalysis." *International Journal of Psycho-Analysis*, 1950, *31*, 78–80.

Kohut, H. *The Restoration of the Self*. New York: International Universities Press, 1977.

Kohut, H. "How Does Analysis Cure?" In A. Goldberg and P. Stepansky (eds.), *How Does Analysis Cure?* Chicago: University of Chicago Press, 1984.

Koss, M. P. "Length of Psychotherapy for Clients Seen in Private Practice." *Journal of Consulting and Clinical Psychology*, 1979, *47* (1), 210–212.

Kramer, S. "The Termination Process in Open-Ended Psychotherapy: Guidelines for Clinical Practice." *Psychotherapy*, 1986, *23* (4), 526–531.

Krebs, R. L. "Client-Centered Therapy—When and How It Should End." *Psychotherapy: Theory, Research and Practice*, 1972, *9* (4), 359–360.

Levenson, E. A. "Problems in Terminating Psychoanalysis (A Symposium): The Aesthetics of Termination." *Contemporary Psychoanalysis*, 1976, *12* (3), 338–342.

Levinson, H. L. "Termination in Psychotherapy: Some Salient Issues." *Social Casework*, Oct. 1977, pp. 480–489.

Levitt, E. *Clinical Research Designs and Analysis.* Springfield, Ill.: Charles Thomas, 1961.

Lipton, S. "The Last Hour." *Journal of the American Psychoanalytic Association*, 1961, *9*, 325–330.

Lowenberg, F. M. *Fundamentals of Social Intervention.* New York: Columbia University Press, 1977.

Masterman, J. F. *Psychotherapy of the Borderline Adult.* New York: Brunner/Mazel, 1976.

Nunberg, H. "Evaluation of the Results of Psychoanalytic Treatment." *International Journal of Psycho-Analysis*, 1954, *35*, 2–7.

Perlman, H. H. "The Problem-Solving Model in Social Casework." In R. W. Roberts and R. H. Nee (eds.), *Theories of Social Casework.* Chicago: University of Chicago Press, 1970.

Pumpian-Mindlin, E. "Comments on Techniques of Termination and Transfer in a Clinic Setting." *American Journal of Psychotherapy*, 1955, *12*, 455–464.

Rank, O. "The Trauma of Birth in Its Importance to Psychoanalytic Therapy." *Psychoanalytic Review*, 1924, *2* (3), 241–245.

Rank, O. *Will Therapy and Truth and Reality.* New York: Knopf, 1945.

Rank, O. *The Trauma of Birth.* New York: R. Brunner, 1952.

Rapoport, L. "Crisis Intervention as a Mode of Brief Treatment." In R. W. Roberts and R. H. Nee (eds.), *Theories of Social Casework.* Chicago: University of Chicago Press, 1970.

Raskin, N., and Rogers, C. *Person-Centered Therapy in Current Psychotherapies*. (4th ed.) R. Corsini and D. Wedding (eds.). Itasca, Ill.: Peacock, 1989.

Reich, T. "On the Termination of Analysis." In *Psychoanalytic Contributions*. New York: International Universities Press, 1973.

Reid, W. J., and Epstein, L. *Task-Centered Casework*. New York: Columbia University Press, 1972.

Robbins, W. S. "Termination: Problems and Techniques." *Journal of the American Psychoanalytic Association*, 1975, *23*, 166-176.

Rogers, C. *Counseling and Psychotherapy*. Boston: Houghton Mifflin, 1942.

Rogers, C. *Client-Centered Therapy*. Boston: Houghton Mifflin, 1951.

Rogers, C. *On Becoming a Person*. Boston: Houghton Mifflin, 1961.

Rossner, J. *August*. New York: Warner Books, 1983.

Saul, L. *Psychodynamically Based Psychotherapy*. New York: Science House, 1972.

Schafer, R. "The Termination of Brief Psychoanalytic Psychotherapy." *International Journal of Psychoanalytic Psychotherapy*, 1973, *2* (12), 135-148.

Schiff, S. K. "Termination of Therapy." *Archives of General Psychiatry*, 1962, *6* (1), 93-98.

Siporin, M. *Introduction to Social Work Practice*. New York: Macmillan, 1975.

Smalley, R. *Theory of Social Work Practice*. New York: Columbia University Press, 1967.

Taft, J. *Otto Rank: A Biographical Study*. New York: Julian Press, 1958.

Taft, J. "Review of Rank's Technique." *Journal of the Rank Association*, 1966, *1* (1), 66-88.

Weigert, E. "Contribution to the Problem of Terminating Psychoanalyses." *Psychoanalytic Quarterly*, 1952, *21*, 465-480.

Wolberg, L. R. *The Technique of Psychotherapy*. New York: Grune & Stratton, 1972.

Index